Some Cotswold Country Houses

FRONTISPIECE

Dyrham Park. The approach downhill to the east front.
All that remains of the Dutch-style garden
is the foreground figure of Neptune c. 1700.

JAMES LEES-MILNE

Some Cotswold Country Houses

THE DOVECOTE PRESS

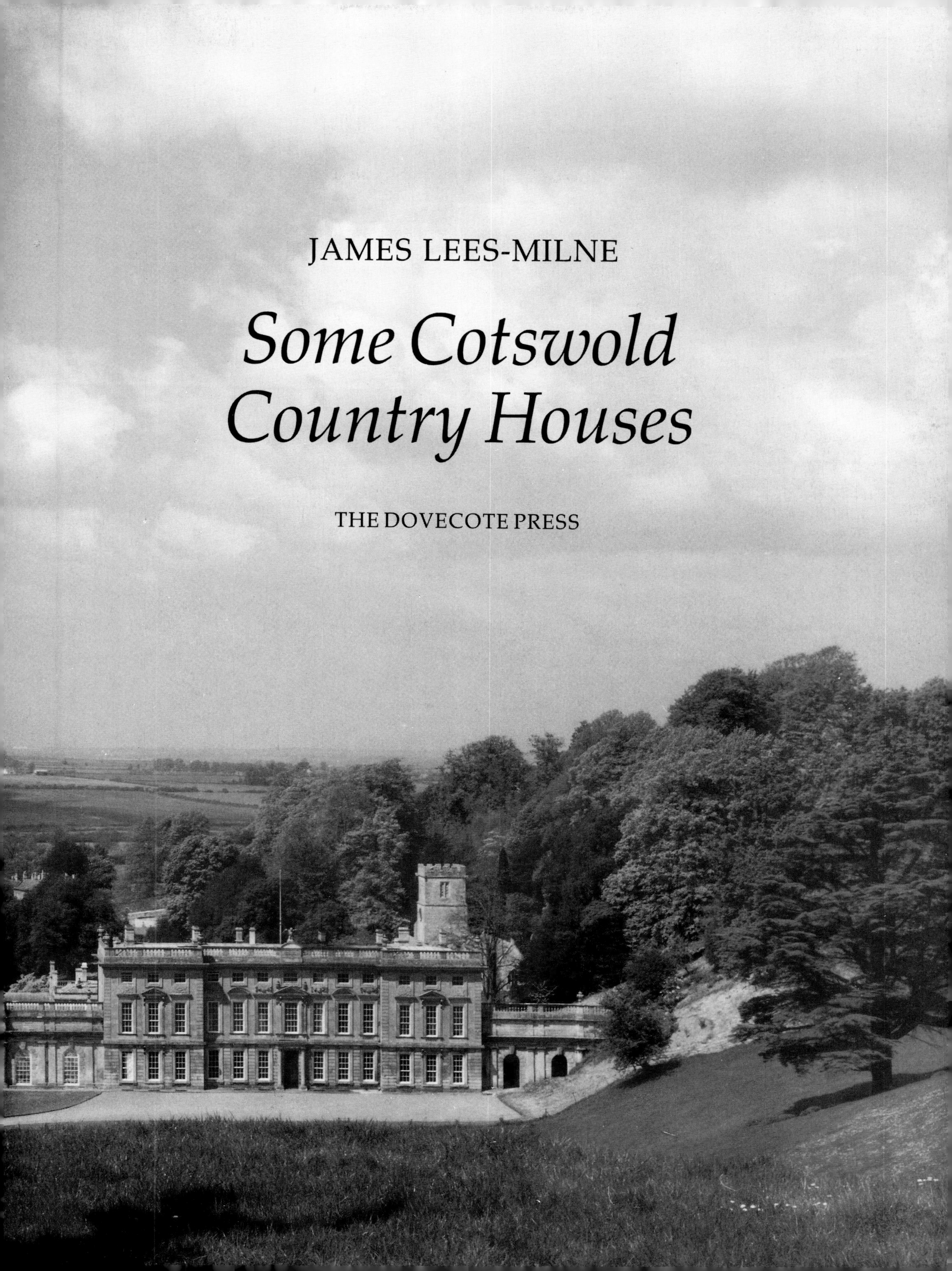

First published in 1987 by The Dovecote Press Ltd.
Stanbridge, Wimborne, Dorset BH21 4JD
ISBN 0 946159 45 9

Designed by Humphrey Stone

Photoset in Palatino by
Character Graphics, Taunton, Somerset
Film origination and assembly by Aero Offset,
Bournemouth, Dorset
Printed and bound in Great Britain by
Biddles Ltd, Guildford and King's Lynn

Contents

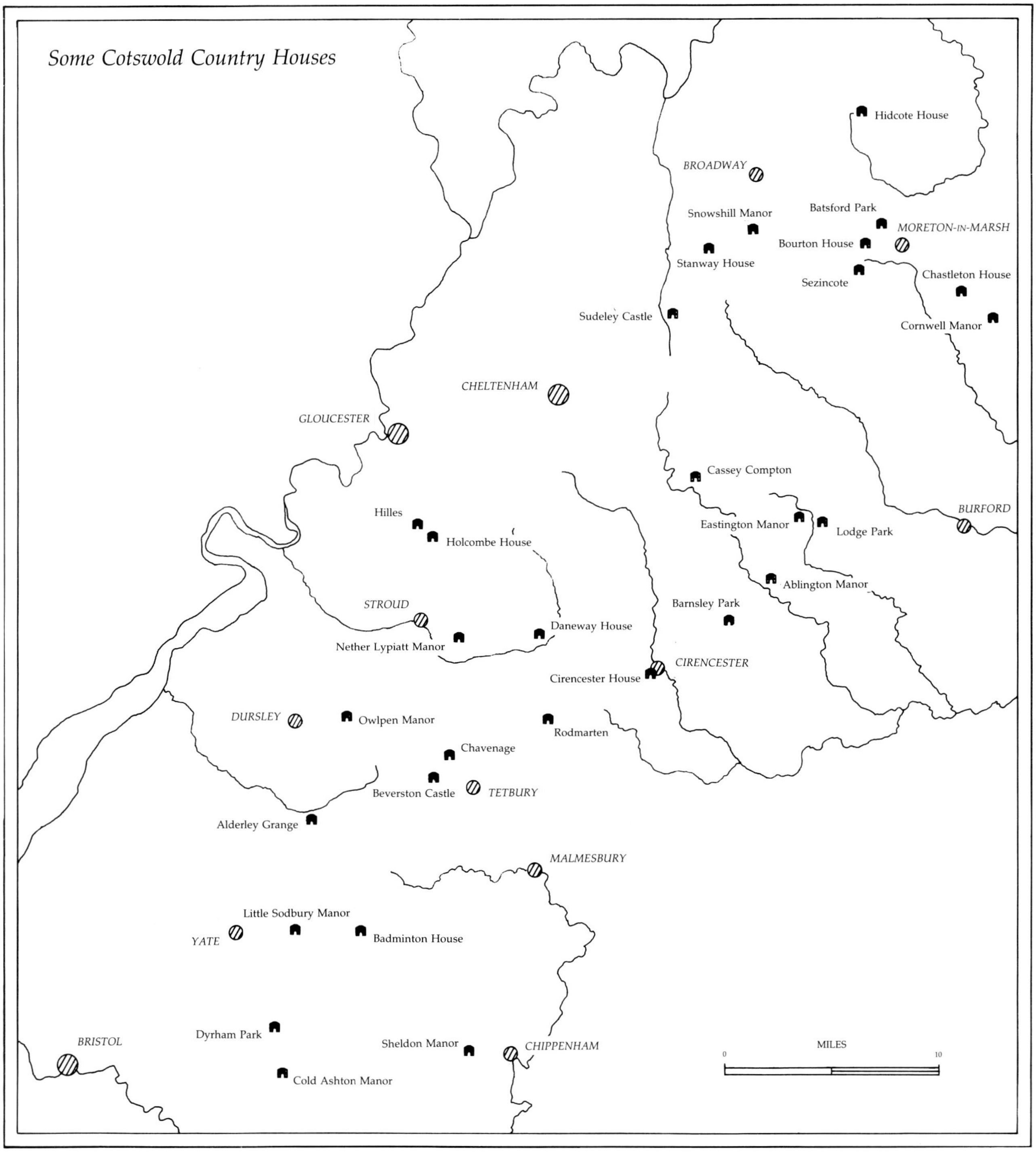

Some Cotswold Country Houses
Hidcote House
BROADWAY
Snowshill Manor
Batsford Park
MORETON-IN-MARSH
Bourton House
Stanway House
Sezincote
Chastleton House
Sudeley Castle
Cornwell Manor
CHELTENHAM
GLOUCESTER
Cassey Compton
BURFORD
Hilles
Eastington Manor
Lodge Park
Holcombe House
Ablington Manor
STROUD
Barnsley Park
Daneway House
Nether Lypiatt Manor
CIRENCESTER
Cirencester House
DURSLEY
Owlpen Manor
Rodmarten
Chavenage
Beverston Castle
TETBURY
Alderley Grange
MALMESBURY
Little Sodbury Manor
YATE
Badminton House
Dyrham Park
Sheldon Manor
BRISTOL
CHIPPENHAM
Cold Ashton Manor
MILES
0
10

Introduction

This book is a sort of sequel – however unworthy – to the late Lord David Cecil's delightful volume, *Some Dorset Country Houses.* The same principles and problems which beset him have confronted me. As he pointed out in his Foreword the *Some* in the title must be borne in mind by the indulgent reader. In one sense my task of selection has been more difficult than his because the Cotswolds – which chiefly mean Gloucestershire – are even more abundant in country houses than Dorset. In another sense my task has been easier in that I have not been restricted, and maddened, by the recent idiotic tampering with the age-old county boundaries. Fortunately the Cotswolds transcend boundaries, old and new, and spill over into other counties beyond Gloucestershire. In actual fact I have included two houses in Oxfordshire and one in Wiltshire.

A definition of the Cotswolds as a region has proved in my case insoluble. As I have indicated in the text their extent from north to south and indeed to the west is easily determined. In the north and south the land subsides neatly into flat terrain. On the west the long escarpment separating highlands from the vale makes a still more rigid boundary. But when we come to the east, where on earth do the Cotswolds end? There is no abrupt declivity and the limestone belt which characterises the Cotswolds so radically continues right across England. Now whereas it would be patently absurd to pronounce that Burghley House, Stamford, was within our region, houses nearer home so to speak are a questionable matter. I was sorely tempted to include beautiful and interesting Broughton Castle, near Banbury (had the owner been willing), but decided regretfully that it was perhaps beyond our pale.

Having resolved this dilemma other hydra heads naturally arose. Throughout the Medieval, Tudor and Stuart periods the Cotswolds were the most prosperous region of the British Isles, outside the cities. It is a truism to state that most Cotswold country houses were the outcome of sheep breeders' and wool merchants' fortunes. They are as numerous as they are appealing. How therefore to choose between them? My choice was limited by certain factors. Some houses, like Adlestrop Park, Northwick Park and Sandywell Park, vacated by their previous owners, have been put to different uses to those for which they were built. Westonbirt House, surely the grandest Victorian mansion, is, although well maintained, a girls' school.

My objective has been to include large and small, ancient and modern country houses, that is to say representatives of every period and style from the Middle Ages down to 1939 – I know of none after that date – provided they are still privately owned. At once I must confess to two exceptions – in the National Trust-owned Dyrham Park and Snowshill Manor. The principal rooms at Dyrham are so beautifully shown that the Blathwayt family might still be in residence; besides the lesser rooms and outbuildings provide some half a dozen self-contained flats, with the result that this large house is a very living concern. As for Snowshill, an astonishing magpie's nest of antiquities and bric-a-brac, it was never exactly a private house even when privately inhabited within living memory. I do not apologize for their inclusion. Exceptions, like white lies, oil the wheels of civilized society.

The variety of houses chosen is, I like to think, distinctive. Badminton may be a palace and Eastington Manor a yeoman's dwelling; Sudeley Castle a rebuilt ruin, and Cassey Compton a fraction of a long-since demolished whole. Stanway is a large house scarcely altered since being built in Tudor and Jacobean times; Nether Lypiatt Manor is all of a piece, early Georgian; so too is Barnsley Park, which is mid-Georgian; and Sezincote, which is Regency and very eccentric to boot; and Batsford Park, out and in Victorian. There is nothing at Daneway later than James I's reign and nothing at Rodmarton earlier than George V's. Lodge Park is so minute that it almost qualifies for the subject of Horace Walpole's gibe when he first saw Chiswick Villa: it is too small to live in and too large to hang on one's watch-chain.

Every old house in the Cotswolds was built of oolite stone; no other building materials were eligible. Here again the variety of Cotswold stone is remarkable. Nearly every quarry, and fifty years ago hundreds were being worked (now there are at most three), yielded stone of its own subtle colouring. So we have numerous shades of grey, mauve, cream, buff, honey, yellow and even orange. Of them all I think the Guiting quarry yields the most striking stone, a mixture of honey and Jersey butter, especially when silvered over with the lichen of that area. Stanway is built of Guiting stone and even in the dreariest weather, when the skies are low and leaden, this most beautiful of country houses suffuses its surroundings with light.

Most, but not all, of the houses in this book I have known over a lifetime. Some I had not visited for years, and it was interesting to see how the present owners, several of whom are the sons, grandsons or great-nephews of my original hosts, to put it bluntly, cope. The majority do so extraordinarily well, with staffs reduced to skeleton dimensions, or none at all. The number of large houses in which there are no resident servants is considerable, making me wonder how on earth those domestic armies in pre-Great War days were able to fill in their time. Indeed, a long retired indoor servant at Westonbirt once solemnly assured me that, when engaged by Sir George Holford in the 1920s as hall-boy, his duties consisted of keeping the wood fire stoked, providing fresh blotting-paper and putting new nibs into penholders. Nothing more.

Many large country houses have either been demolished or turned into unsuitable institutions. The last fate seems to me often worse than the first because, denuded of contents and replaced with steel filing-cabinets and computers, or school desks, the fine rooms lose their ethos and their souls. Besides, institutions usually add unsightly excrescences (on the cheap) resembling factories or *public conveniences*. One would rather be left with a good photograph of what such a house looked like in its prime.

It is rare to find a country house where butler or parlour-maid is employed; and rare enough to find a permanent cook. The trained housemaid is absolutely extinct. Even so the cherished 'daily' can keep the few inhabited rooms fairly clean, and dustsheets are adequate protectors of furnished yet unused rooms. There are far worse menaces than clean country dust.

On the other hand it is astonishing how quickly the Cotswold manor-houses get snapped up as soon as they come on the market. The most isolated village is today no longer too remote for the commuter, as the waggon-wheels on cottage walls and carriage lamps flanking the front doors testify. The commuter invasion is an inevitable sequel to the recent network of motorways. No manor-house with a few paddocks seems too expensive. This would be all to the good were the new commuter-squire to settle. But unfortunately he seldom does for long. One very desirable house which, when I visited it during the Second World War, was occupied by the last of a line of hereditary owners, has since changed hands eight times. Each successive owner, however good his intentions and his taste, inevitably makes alterations and something vanishes from the house. Likewise by ceaseless change of the geographical scene – more pylons, more cables, fewer dry-stone walls and hedges, meaning more barbed wire and pig wire, more community tips, more agricultural Dutch and fewer traditional barns, more developers' bungalows of reconstructed stone, and ever more concrete and less grass – the ambience of the best preserved country house can be ruined. On this disgruntled note I must pause to reflect.

The fact is that of the twenty-eight country houses I have been privileged to describe in these pages the immediate surroundings of one only can be said to have deteriorated slightly, thanks to the pride and loving care of the owners.

To these owners I am immensely indebted for permission to include their houses. Every one has been kind, hospitable, helpful and tolerant. I think it extraordinary that no single owner whom I approached has said *No*. One only did not reply, and of him, sensible man, I subsequently learnt that he could neither read nor write.

At first I considered giving a list of all those learned authorities from whom I have gleaned much information. On reflection, that seemed pretentious in a personal book of this sort. In the text I have referred to specific authors when I have either quoted or paraphrased them. Otherwise the opinions expressed are my own.

Finally, there is my friend David Burnett. The idea of this book was his. The production of it is as much his as mine. We have worked together in sympathy and harmony. No wonder I am grateful because he has been chauffeur, plotter of routes, map-reader, path-finder (in the Cotswolds a far more awkward matter than a non-Cotswold dweller may suppose), brusher-aside of all obstacles, inspirer of enthusiasms, sharer of jokes, as well as chief photographer, editor and single-handed publisher. How he has managed to combine all these roles with unvarying good humour and efficiency is more than I can understand. I thank him most sincerely.

J.L–M.

Ablington Manor. The south or garden front today, seen across the river Coln.

Ablington Manor

J. Arthur Gibbs (1868-1899).

'How well I remember the first time I came upon it! One fine September evening, having left all traces of railways and the ancient town of Cirencester some seven long miles behind me, with wearied limbs I sought this quiet, sequestered spot... Below me was a small village, nestling amid a wealth of stately trees. The hand of many seemed in some byegone time to have done all that was necessary to render the place habitable, but no more...

I was enchanted with the place. The quaint old Elizabethan gables and sombre bell-tower, the old-fashioned entrance gates, the luxuriant growth of ivy, combined together to give that air of peace, that charm which belongs so exclusively to the buildings of the middle ages. Knowing that the house was for the time being unoccupied, I walked boldly into the outer porch, meaning to go no further. But another inscription over the solid oak door encouraged me to enter:

Porta patens esto, nulli claudaris Honesto.

I therefore entered the inner door with some difficulty, for it was heavy and cumbersome, and found myself in the hall. I was delighted to find everything in keeping with the place. The old-fashioned furniture, the old oak, the grim portraits and quaint heraldry, all were there...

I was told that the place was still owned by the descendants of the pious John Coxwell who built the manor house and commemorated it by the quaint inscription over the porch in 1590.'

Who was this person who had trudged from Cirencester railway station on foot to Ablington, and wrote so rapturously about what he found on his journey's end? By the repetition of the adjective *quaint* one guesses at once that he did not belong to our age. Joseph Arthur Gibbs was a young man in his 'twenties, a member of the Gibbs clan of merchants and bankers and through his mother, a relation of his namesake Arthur Hallam, the subject of Tennyson's *In Memoriam*. Indeed Arthur Gibbs bore some resemblance to this immortalized paragon of early 19th-century manhood, to whose 'god-like charm' he referred. At Eton Arthur Gibbs' tutor was Henry Luxmoore who thought the world of his literary promise. And at Christ Church, Oxford he distinguished himself at work and athletics. But it was nature which at an early age captivated him; and after nature sport.

The long and the short of the high-minded young man's walk to Ablington that September afternoon in the 1890's was that he rented the manor house, lived in it, loved it, got to know the surrounding country like the back of his hand, and died tragically young in 1899 at the age of thirty-one. By this uneventful passage through life he would not be remembered today, had he not written and published the year before his death a book which has become a minor, certainly a provincial classic, called *A Cotswold Village*.

Arthur Gibbs simply soused himself in the Cotswold ways of life and traditions. Although some of his descriptive prose reads sentimentally to us, he was under no illusions about the poverty of agricultural workers and the ruthlessness of nature, every phase of which he studied with a clinical eye. Nor was he so besotted by the beauty of the country he had adopted as to view it through rose-tinted spectacles. 'To anyone who might be thinking of becoming for the time being "a tourist",' he wrote, 'and in that capacity visiting the Cotswolds, my advice is "Don't". There is really nothing to see. There is nothing, that is to say, which may not be seen much nearer London.' At times one is tempted to wish that posterity had heeded his advice, so crowded are the Cotswolds throughout the summer. As it is *A Cotswold Village* was one of the first books to popularise the district, creating a portrait of the Cotswolds as a rural idyll, England at its most perfect, a view that still casts its spell today.

Ablington is strictly speaking a hamlet in the parish of Bibury, where it sprawls along the banks of the most beautiful of the Cotswold rivers, the Coln. 'The pious John Coxwell', who acquired land at Ablington and built the manor house, was a member of a rich wool merchant family. He was also a munificent benefactor of St John the Baptist's noble church at Cirencester, where the family owned property and a street is named after him.

John Coxwell's Ablington Manor is built practically on the village street and hidden by a high wall. One entrance is through a pair of imposing stone piers with balls giving on to a back court. The other employs the river and a two-arched bridge to add to its charm, beyond which the Coln suddenly widens and flows swiftly between the garden and some low-lying marshland backed by a steep bank of trees, whilst the drive sweeps on past lawns and an elephantine yew hedge with feet of box.

No wonder young Mr Gibbs was taken with it for it is exactly the sort of manor-house one associates with the Cotswolds. Although other parts of the house have been slightly altered within the past ninety years or so, the north side has not changed at all – as the line engraving in *A Cotswold Village* indicates. Here are three pointed gables with a finial on each apex, apparently bending backwards like the prows of three old men-of-war buffeted by the waves of time. The walls of rubble are sheathed with harling of yellow ochre wash, patchy, mottled and enchanting. From a lower wing to the left rises a Georgian cupola like a mushroom on thin stalks. It once sheltered a bell with which to summon the family to meals or the children to bed. The projecting porch is the show

The double arched bridge which carries the drive over the river Coln.

Ablington Manor, the north front, engraved for the first edition of *A Cotswold Village*.

Ablington Manor. Old annexe, including pigeon loft, to east of the garden front, from within the pergola garden.

Detail of the front door frieze, showing primitive heads possibly representing Edward VI, Henry VIII and Elizabeth I.

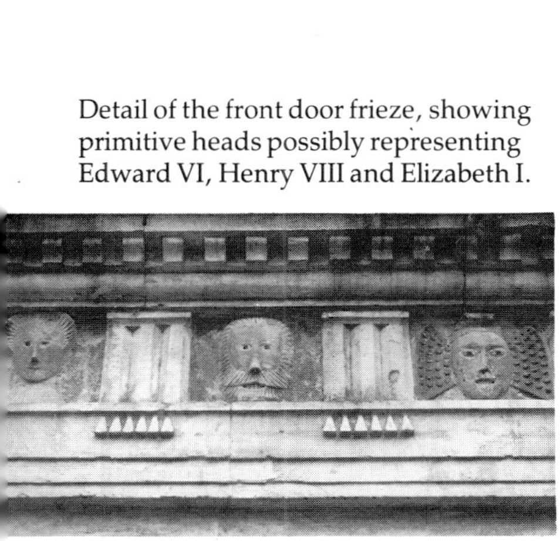

piece of the ancient composition. It is of dressed stone and bears the date "Anno Domeney 1590", just two years after the defeat of the Spanish Armada when England was at one of her apexes of power and prosperity. An inscription, 'plead thou my Cause O Lord' may have led Arthur Gibbs to suppose John Coxwell was more spiritual than worldly minded. Devout or not the wool merchant was certainly long-lived for he died in 1614 at the age of 92. Over the entrance are two odd disks carved almost in the round. The doorway outline is not in the Gothic but the advanced Renaissance classical style. Nevertheless the frieze bears five grotesque carved heads, by contrast primitive. The central one with wide ruff is clearly meant to represent Queen Elizabeth I. On either side of her is a bearded man, perhaps rude likenesses of Henry VIII; the remaining two are possibly Edward VI and Bloody Mary. Their background shows traces of blue paint. The front door is fortified by sturdy iron straps and bears a lion knocker.

To the right of the porch is a massive chimney breast; and to the right of it a big stone mask from the mouth of which, man or lion, rain water flows into a hopper head.

The south or garden front likewise has three gables with urn finials on the apex. They look so Elizabethan that only an expert would unhesitantly pronounce them neo-Georgian, for they were alterations done by the Martyr family who bought Ablington from the Coxwell-Rogers family of Dowdeswell in 1920. A photograph of about 1890 shows this front with sashed windows and between the two outer gables a recess with a little token Georgian pediment over a tall window to light the staircase behind it. On the corner of an adjacent annexe is scratched 'Coxwell 1766'. The garden front might be of any period. Ablington Manor is a sort of running commentary on traditional Cotswold building methods and styles.

The interior has been a good deal altered, but not so extensively that Arthur Gibbs would not recognize most of the rooms. The hall, entered from the porch, has been given a duplicate opening in the facing wall to bring more light from the staircase window. The stairs themselves are late Georgian with rather high and extremely slender balusters. It was from the window of the oak panelled 'little room' that in the cool of the evening Arthur watched the wonders of creation in the garden – a moorhen followed by her brood of five little balls of black feather, a thrush sitting on the ivy-clad bough of a tree, scores of rabbits running into the nettles, and out of the river may-flies rising and soaring round the topmost branches of the firs. I wonder if the trout are as copious today as they seem to have been in the 1890's.

Ablington Manor, the south front as it was when J. A. Gibbs lived here. From a photograph taken about 1890.

The present owner, Robert Cooper, has made many improvements to the garden. Along the high wall which bounds the sloping lawn to the river he has contrived a wide bed with a serpentine walk of flagstones. On the far side of the wall a pergola garden has been laid out on a generous scale with the help of the eminent horticulturist, Rosemary Verey.

The two enormous barns on the opposite side of the village street were once filled with the wool that brought the Coxwells their wealth. One is buttressed like a church without a tower. The great nave has two projecting entrances for waggons, and a lower adjunct like a chancel. A date-stone is inscribed I.C. 1727, a year possibly when the medieval roof was restored.

Medieval barn, restored in 1727, on the far side of the road.

Alderley Grange

Alderley is a very small village. Were it not for its church it would be a hamlet since it has no pub, no post-office and no shop. It straddles a spur of the Cotswolds, two miles south of Wotton-under-Edge, between two brooks in the coombes of Killcott and Ozleworth. Whereas Alderley House (now Rosehill, a boys' preparatory school) by Lewis Vulliamy looks south across Kilcott brook, the Grange so-called (pretentiously and without any justification) is sited over Ozleworth coombe or Bottom. Until mid-Victorian times it was known modestly as West End House.

Although the upgraded Grange is of medium size it has a distinct claim to fame in being the birth-place in 1609 of one of Gloucestershire's most renowned sons, Sir Matthew Hale. He became Lord Chief Justice in the reign of Charles II and his memory is still revered as much for his moral qualities as his legal achievements. With scrupulous impartiality he defended Archbishop Laud during his impeachment in 1643. John Aubrey tells a story which illustrates the esteem in which his contemporaries held him.

'About 1646 Mr. John Maynard (now Sir John and Serjeant) came into Middle Temple Hall from Westminster Hall weary with business, and hungry, when [we] had newly dined... We asked Mr. Maynard what was the difference between a just man and a good man. He was beginning to eat and cryed: "Hoh!" He had eate but a bit or two when he reply'd: "I'le tell you the difference presently: Serjeant Rolle is *a just man*, and Matthew Hale is *a good man*," and so fell to make an end of his dinner. And there could not be a better interpretation of this text. For Serjeant Rolle was just but by nature penurious... Matthew Hale was not only just, but wonderfully charitable and open handed, and did not sound a trumpet neither, as the hypocrites doe.'

Sir Mathew Hale, Lord Chief Justice, who was born in the house in 1609.

Deeply devout and a pillar of the Church of England Sir Matthew was fairly tolerant of others' religious opinions. At his death in 1676 he left behind a quantity of religious tracts and precepts, which were posthumously printed and for generations to come widely circulated. At the same time this virtuous and wise man was responsible for convicting in 1661 two poor old women for witchcraft. It was alleged that they had caused children to be overtaken with fainting fits, to vomit nails and pins, and to see mice, ducks and flies which were invisible to adults. A toad ran out of their bed and on being thrown into the fire exploded like the crack of a pistol. The last evidence was in the Judge's view proof positive. Hale sentenced the old women to death by fire at the stake. They were the last witches in England to be thus dealt with.

The bedroom in which Matthew Hale is said to have first seen the light is on the first floor of a wing facing south. It contains a stone Jacobean fireplace. In the middle of the outside wall is a plaque with the date 1608, the year before the future Lord Chief Justice's birth. There is no reason to suppose this is not the original part of the house, the entrance to which was from an existing but no longer used doorway on the north side. At all events the house was extended and given a new look, indeed a new front facing west in the 1740's.

West End House did not pass with the rest of the Alderley estate to Sir Matthew's son and male issue, but to a daughter. Thenceforth it belonged to different owners until the Hales reabsorbed it in the estate at the beginning of this century. The daughter's descendants sold it to a Bristol merchant of Quaker origin, called William Springett. He was a man of means who amassed property at Kilcott and Wickwar. He married about 1744 a daughter of Richard Osborne of Wortley House, which is half a mile to the north of Alderley. Osborne was the proprietor of the largest and most flourishing of fifteen woollen mills working on the Ozleworth brook.

Springett clearly intended to turn West End House into an up-to-date miniature gentleman's seat. And who can deny that the Bristol merchant failed in his ambition? A little to the north and below the house on the slope of Ozleworth Bottom he raised a coach-house for two carriages and loose boxes, ashlar-faced with a crowning pediment. Still more impressive was his house's new entrance front, of very handsome design, consisting of two storeys and an attic floor behind a panelled parapet. Dormer windows can just be detected under the sloping roof. On the first floor the projecting centrepiece was given a pediment over a smart *Venetian* window with blocked surrounds in the manner of James Gibbs. No architect as illustrious as Gibbs worked for Springett, who probably commissioned a local mason with a working knowledge of Gibb's famous *Book of Architecture* of 1728. Michael Sidnell from Bristol was such a person. Described as statuary mason he carved a memorial tablet in Alderley church in 1732. By 1742-5 he had risen to architect and was making designs at the Court House, Westbury-on-Severn, for Maynard Colchester. The precise date of the Alderley front is unrecorded but probably coincided with Springett's marriage. The pedimented porch was a slightly later addition – the date 1751 is scratched on the lead roof – after the Springetts had experienced a decade of the westerly gales that blow from the Bristol Channel. The porch leads to a central hall with stone paving and wide three-flight staircase of alternate plain and twisted balusters and

Top. Alderley Grange, the west front added in the 1740s.

Bottom left. The porch, an addition of 1751.

Bottom right. The staircase in the centre of the mid-Georgian front.

Georgian coach house and stable block.

dado, all of oak. It is a handsome apartment, equal in dimensions to the two front rooms on either side before they were extended.

The only surviving letter of William Springett does not present him in a very attractive light. It is addressed, 'From my small house at Westends September 22nd 1770,' to the lately retired rector of Alderley. It roundly abuses the rector for ingratitude for past condescensions, for not returning a book borrowed five years previously, and for calling – wise man – on the Springetts when he knew they were away from home. 'So it is,' the letter concludes, 'that when men from a low estate are once exalted, they generally are most forgetful of past favours... which is now become too fashionable, especially with such who cover their guilt with the mask of religion... I have been and still am (tho' I don't want any of your assistance) Your very humble servant.' Who on earth did the newly rich merchant Springett think he was? It is disappointing to learn that the chastened rector wrote a grovelling reply.

William Springett died in 1772, leaving all his properties and a fortune to an only daughter Anne, married to Matthew A'Deane who carried on business as a clothier at one of the mills in the parish. The A'Deanes added about 1810 to the ground floor the two single-storey bays of which the outer windows are dummies. Consequently the drawing room and the library on either side of the front door were appreciably lengthened. The simple cornices and reeded moulds of the doorways have a Regency flavour.

From 1867 until 1894 the house was owned by a man of great distinction whose name is not familiar today. Brian Houghton Hodgson, F.R.S. was an Indian civilian, orientalist and botanist. For twenty-three years (1820-43) he was assistant-resident in Nepal where he devoted himself to the study of the literature, religion and languages of a country then totally unknown. He acquired original Sanscrit manuscripts and copies of others which he distributed among public libraries in Calcutta, Paris and London. Further manuscripts he donated to the India Office. A pioneer of scientific ethnology he was also a zoologist and biologist of note. He introduced to this country a rhododendron called after him *Hodgsoni*, and finally presented to the British Museum more than 10,000 specimens of birds, mammals and reptiles and 1800 drawings to the Zoological Society. From the age of 67 to 94 he settled with his second wife at the Grange, loaded with honours from many countries except his own.

Indeed towards the end of the last century Alderley village became quite an intellectual centre. At the big house lived two un-married brothers, General Robert and Colonel Matthew Holford Hale, both distinguished soldiers and cultivated men. At the Mount House, a short walk from the Grange, Marianne North, the intrepid traveller and artist spent the last years of her life from 1885-1890. Here she wrote her *Recollections* and from here founded the Marianne North Gallery at Kew. Here she was visited by her many

Georgian summerhouse with segmental pediment and contemporary bench made to fit.

Alderley Grange, the west front. A detail from a recent painting by Graham Rust.

relations including her brother-in-law John Addington Symonds, the poet and art historian. Hodgson too had numerous well known friends to stay. In listing Sir Joseph Hooker, Friedrich Max Müller, Arthur Grote and T.H. Huxley, Hodgson's biographer wrote that they 'were a few of the men of note who made Alderley Grange unique in its way among English country homes.'

A doorway to the right of the main facade leads to the double walled garden at the rear of the house. The walls are basically of stone, those to the south and west being faced with brick the better to conserve the heat of the sun for fruit. A Georgian segmental gazebo with Chippendale-style seat shaped to fit confronts an ancient mulberry tree under which the nonagenarian Hodgson would in summer sit at a little table enriching the margins of his books with erudite notes. The garden with its lawns, umbrageous trees, lime walks, herb gardens and rampageous old-fashioned roses flourishes in the loving care of its present owners Mr and the Hon. Mrs Guy Acloque.

Badminton House

Badminton House, entrance to the north forecourt.

Top. Staghunting at Badminton. One of a series of canvases by John Wootton of the 3rd Duke of Beaufort now hanging in the Hall.

Middle. Badminton House, the north front, from the painting by Canaletto in 1749.

Bottom. Badminton House, the north front, begun c. 1660 and altered by Gibbs and Kent.

Badminton has always been the grandest seat in Gloucestershire. With its vast estates it is still a sort of principality, still with a reigning duke. Yet there is an unaccountable homeliness about it. It is approached through the pretty village with its colour-washed cottages, past some rather unducal gates, down a short drive leading to an outer court where the cars are washed, under a stable arch, through another open courtyard with a *porte cochère* on one side and a duckpond on the other, under an impressive William Kent pavilion, and into the forecourt. This route suggests having crossed a frontier, of having entered a Ruritanian kingdom whose capital is the village and palace the house. And what a palace! The state rooms may fill its heart, but there are kitchens and sculleries and little pantries in profusion. One corridor leads into another, to emerge without warning into a shadowy landing or at the foot of a staircase. Boots and hunting crops may overflow in one room, paintings or bookshelves line the walls of the next. And from the windows along the spreading mass of the north front there are views of a dead-straight avenue nearly three miles long that ends at the arch of the most beautiful lodge in England.

The 1st Duke of Beaufort was one of Charles II's creations, although not of his procreations. Yet his origins were just as royal. The 1st Duke was a descendant of the 1st Earl of Worcester. The 1st Earl, created in 1514 by Henry VIII, was the illegitimate son of Henry Beaufort, Duke of Somerset (hence the family surname and the confusion), who in turn was a great-grandson of John of Gaunt. In other words the Dukes of Beaufort are Plantagenets in the direct male line. And the Plantagenets were far more illustrious than the Tudors who married into the Somerset branch. It was in right of his mother Margaret Beaufort that Henry VII claimed the throne of England in 1485.

For four hundred years Badminton had been owned by the Boteler family. In 1608 it was bought by the 4th Earl of Worcester for his second son, Thomas Somerset, who promptly transformed it into a Jacobean mansion. Thomas's unmarried daughter left it to her cousin, afterwards 1st Duke of Beaufort, in 1655. Until then the Lords Worcester had lived at Raglan Castle, Monmouthshire, which was acquired by the 1st Earl's first wife, in her own right

Lady Herbert of Raglan. The gift of Badminton was doubtless very welcome since Raglan Castle had been 'slighted' by the Parliamentarians during the Civil War. Needless to say the Duke's father had been a staunch King's man who suffered grievously for his loyalty. He was also a man of rare inventiveness who published a book in which, according to Burke's Peerage, 'the power and application of the steam engine are distinctly described.' He also nearly succeeded in making an artificial bird fly, chirp and even hover.

On his acquisition of Badminton the 3rd Marquess (not yet Duke) began transforming the Botelers' rambling and gabled house into a palace. He tackled the east and north fronts, temporarily leaving the old south and west fronts more or less as they were. The north or entrance front he built up to the present cornice. It was an early essay at the Palladian style and if not by Inigo Jones, may have been designed by that great man's disciple, John Webb. At the rear of his new classical front the 3rd Marquess refashioned a range of rooms subsequently altered. Of these the oak room takes its name from elaborate dark panelling brought in 1895 from Troy House, another Somerset seat near Monmouth. The dining-room was embellished with Grinling Gibbons carving after the 3rd Marquess became Duke in 1682. The pilasters, cornice and doorcases of this remarkable room were almost certainly the work of Edward Poynton, a gentleman carver of Nottingham in 1732, who imparted a distinct Rococo flavour.

Evidently the 1st Duke's chief concern was his park. The terrain being pancake flat enabled him to work on a gigantic scale. He made the house the nucleus of thirty straight rides which were intersected by some 24 others radiating from a *rond-point* to the south-east. Although William Kent designed 'an improvement on Ye Lawn' in 1745 and Capability Brown was paid in 1752 for plans for various landscape alterations, all of which came to nothing, the lesser known Thomas Wright of Durham left a more positive impression on the surroundings of Badminton. He too made a number of landscape suggestions which again were ignored, but he did carry out several ornamental park buildings. The 1st Duke's network of rides was smudged by time's inexorable change rather than by the positive hands of improvers. Yet several of his straight rides can still be traced, notably that great survivor, the drive from the north entrance of the house to Worcester Lodge, the east avenue and Centre Walk (actually just off-centre) which stretches obliquely from the south front across the railway and even beyond the M4 motorway. The Duke's extraordinary layout dumbfounded neighbouring landowners. Roger North recorded that 'divers gentlemen cut their trees and hedges to humour his vistos, and some planted their hills in his line, for compliment, at their own charge.'

The 1st Duke died in 1700. His elder son having predeceased him (killed after throwing himself out of a runaway coach) he was

The 1st Duke of Beaufort (1629-1700) and his family. Portrait by Captain S. Browne.

succeeded by his grandson. The 2nd Duke, a strong Tory and Jacobite sympathizer, only survived fourteen years, having achieved little in the building line. His son the 3rd Duke combined a love of sport with the arts. He practically completed the remodelling of the interior begun by his great-grandfather, and left the exterior to all intents and purposes as it is now. For a short period he employed that ubiquitous provincial architect Francis Smith of Warwick on the west and east fronts, even turning Smith's attention to aggrandizing the north front. There exists a letter from the duke to his duchess in which he writes in 1737, 'Smith was here yesterday and shakes his head sadly about a pediment.' The existing walls, he explained, simply would not take the weight of additional stone. However when Smith died in 1738 the Duke engaged the better known Tory and Catholic architect James Gibbs, whom his brother the 4th Duke discarded in favour of William Kent. If Gibbs may have added the pair of wooden cupolas to the north front Kent certainly constructed the rather top-heavy wooden pediment and a third storey to the flanking wings. He also transformed the pair of terminal pavilions, begun by Gibbs, into a concatenation of bold, blocked columns supporting bolder pediments and a pyramidal roof.

It is open to question whether the great entrance hall, intended to take the enormous canvases by John Wootton of the 3rd Duke depicted beagling, hawking, racing and stag-hunting, and of his life-size white Arabian horse over the fireplace, is to Kent's design (indeed Gibbs' is the more likely). At all events the hall is one of the noblest state-rooms in the Cotswolds. It was here during a particularly inclement winter in 1863 that the children of the 8th Duke invented the game of Badminton. Below the great Wootton paintings in their majestic gilt frames stucco trophies of the chase are corded together by draperies held in the mouths of foxes. If this great room is Baroque the octagonal waiting-hall behind it is by contrast a delicate Rococo. The plaster ceiling and walls are the work of Thomas Paty of Bristol in the 1750s. Of the four stately doorways one leads to the grand staircase and the east wing respectively. It is in this wing that the present duke and duchess chiefly reside.

The east side consists of an enfilade of rooms from the library, begun by the 3rd Duke and heightened by Jeffry Wyattville nearly a hundred years later, a beautiful and wholly architectural room, to the great drawing-room in a furthermost wing projecting northwards. The last is dominated by two splendid Italian features. One is a chimneypiece of Carrara marble, porphyry and ormolu, commissioned by the 6th Duchess of Beaufort while in Rome in 1773, and the other a massive cabinet of *pietre dure*, made for the 3rd Duke in Florence in 1732. It stands in the niche designed by Wyatville to contain it. The small drawing-rooms between still retain rich wallpapers designed by Thomas Willement in the 1840s.

The collection throughout the house of Somerset family portraits dating from Tudor times is unrivalled among Gloucestershire families. In addition, the two paintings by Canaletto, one taken

The east front, begun by the 1st Duke, showing extension (right) by Wyatville, and the church (left) of 1785.

Badminton House, the Hall. The painting on the easel by Landseer is of the 8th Duke as a boy standing with his pony in the Hall.

The central block of the east front, heightened by Francis Smith between 1729 and 1738.

from the central upstairs window looking up Worcester Avenue and the other of the north front of the house are treasures beyond compare.

Interior of the church built by Charles Evans under the influence of Gibbs's St Martin-in-the-Fields.

The parish church of Great Badminton, rebuilt in 1785 for the 5th Duke by a little-known London architect called Charles Evans on the lines of St. Martin's-in-the-Fields, but without aisle galleries, is entered from the south-east wing of the house straight into a raised pew, complete with fireplace, for the family, at the west end. It is no longer put to this exclusive use. The church is a veritable museum of the finest English sculptors. There are monuments to successive dukes, that of the 1st vying in magniloquent splendour with any tomb in Westminster Abbey. In fact it came from St. George's Chapel Windsor Castle and is by Grinling Gibbons, the reclining effigy disclosed by parted curtains under the heavenly host with palms and a crown. Gesticulating life-size figures by Gibbons of Justice and Charity were expressly designed to relieve the stiffness and add flamboyance to the composition. The 2nd and 3rd Dukes are commemorated by Rysbrack on a similar scale. Both effigies are clad in Roman military garb, one standing, the other seated. White marble drapery cascades over a black marble sarcophagus on to a plinth recording the princely titles of the deceased. So too is the 4th Duke's effigy standing in a toga likewise by Rysbrack. He was a secret Jacobite who received Prince Charles Stuart on his surreptitious visit to London in 1750. There is a portrait of the Bonnie Prince's wife, known as the Countess of Albany, hanging, as it were apologetically, at the top of the stairs. The 7th Duke was a patron of Landseer who frequently stayed at Badminton and drew little pictures of animals for the amusement of the Somerset children.

In addition to Worcester Lodge, definitely the work of Kent and his clerk of works Stephen Wright, there are a number of fanciful farm buildings and follies still remaining in what was originally a park of nine miles circumference. Others have unfortunately disappeared. Swangrove built in 1701 on a minute scale has one upstairs room approached by outside steps, and four tiny detached pavilions. There is a pair of quaint castellated lodges like Staffordshire pottery ornaments found on cottage chimneypieces, a superb Georgian Castle Barn with battlements and flanking towers, a miniature folly called 'Ragged Castle' and a Root House. These are the work of Thomas Wright of Durham (not known to be a relation of his namesake Stephen) in the middle of the 18th century.

During the Second World War Badminton was the retreat of Queen Mary, the aunt of Mary Duchess of Beaufort. There are sympathetic and amusing accounts of her sojourn in Osbert Sitwell's memoirs and Sir John Colville's *Downing Street Diaries*. Attended by fifty-five servants the venerable Queen Mother lived in state and servitude. She would come down plastered in diamonds to an austerity dinner of thin soup and spam. Bored to tears by the country she regarded her Badminton incarceration as Charles I did his imprisonment in Carisbooke Castle. She much enjoyed giving lifts in her antique Daimler to soldiers which scared them out of their wits and rendered them speechless, hacking ivy off trees and picking up scrap metal for the war effort.

The 10th Duke ('Master') reigned for sixty years until 1984. He was the leading sportsman of the age; master of foxhounds, and Master of the Horse. More learned in fox lore than lettered he was possibly the only man who neither wrote nor even read his own auto-biography. His ground-floor sitting room remains a fitting memorial to his horsemanship, with its equestrian portraits, both of himself and his family in hunting dress, and china figures of horses, foxes and hounds. The present Duke, an internationally recognized expert on paintings has already embellished the village by recolour-washing the houses and cottages, and has planted tens of thousands of trees on the estate. To him the house owes the return of a painting by Landseer showing the 8th Duke standing in the Hall alongside his pony, which he spotted in a saleroom and now hangs in the room in which it was originally painted – chance, perhaps, but one which underlines the sense of continuity Badminton evokes.

Worcester Lodge, by William Kent, c. 1746.

Barnsley Park

Barnsley Park, the west front from an engraving by J. and H. S. Storer published in 1825.

Top. Barnsley Park, the south front.

Bottom left. Centrepiece of the entrance front.

Bottom right. The Hall, richly decorated in the Baroque manner.

When motoring from Cirencester on the Bibury road, one passes through Barnsley, which is immediately noticeable as being unlike any other Cotswold village. It has no outstanding architecture and it is not self-consciously old-world. Yet it leaves one with a feeling of unusual satisfaction. What then is so unusual about it? Owing to the munificence of a rich man, Sir Philip Stott of distant Stanton Court near Broadway, who fell in love with it, there are no unsightly telephone or electricity wires. Between the wars Sir Philip put the wires underground or hid them behind the houses. How he managed to do this, or how since his death, the village has not been extended or spoilt remains a mystery.

Twisting sharply to the right at the north end of the village the road obeys the dictates of a fairly low park wall. Tantalizing ancient trees and an octagonal lodge by John Nash the Regency architect, known as the Pepper Pot, whet the appetite but do not afford a glimpse of the house, which is one of the most unusual and exciting in Gloucestershire. Although Nash had a hand in altering the library and building the orangery in 1807, the house is basically early, not late Georgian, the rainwater heads actually bearing the dates 1720 and 1721. Barnsley Park is certainly the best example of an uncompromisingly Baroque country house in the county. And yet this house, ingeniously planned, superbly built and lavishly decorated, has not yet been attributed with any certainty to a particular architect.

Since rainwater heads are usually the last exterior features to be imposed upon a building the shell of this large house must have been begun before 1713 when Brereton Bourchier died, leaving it to an only daughter, aged 10, by his second marriage. For not till 1719 did she marry a certain Henry Perrot, M.P. for Oxford and a hanger-on at the court of James Brydges, 1st Duke of Chandos, a nobleman of immense riches and a maniac for building. Furthermore, Mrs Perrot's mother had been Catharine Brydges, the Duke's sister. All this may help explain Brereton Bourchier's itch to build at Barnsley where his forebears had settled since Henry VIII's reign. Hence too the resemblances albeit on a humbler scale, between the new Barnsley Park and the Duke of Chandos's great mansion of Cannons, Middlesex, and his designs for his equally great London residence, in Cavendish Square. Although Cannons was demolished in the 18th century and Chandos House was never built, detailed architectural engravings of each survive. The questions still unanswered are did the princely Duke's houses influence the style of Barnsley, as one might expect, or did Barnsley influence the Duke's? And whichever way round it was, who, again, was the architect of Barnsley?

Matters are complicated by the fact that Chandos employed (and sacked) a succession of eminent architects for Cannons – William Talman (1713), John James (1714), Edward Strong (1715), Robert Benson, John Vanbrugh and James Gibbs (1716-19) John Price (1720-1) and even others. The last named is the least known architect of the lot, and yet his published project (1720) for Chandos House bears more resemblances to Barnsley Park, than any of the others'. Besides this, Cannon's dates concur with those of the rainwater heads at Barnsley. Yet another architect, John James, has lately been a favourite but I do not detect any of his quirky conceits, prominent at Appuldurcombe and Warbrooks House. Until scholars reach some definite accord it is best to leave the competition unresolved, and concentrate on the undoubted merits of Barnsley, distinguished as it is by use of the giant order of Corinthian columns, an attic storey above the principal cornice, a flat roof balustrade, and arched windows on the ground floor, all features incidentally found on Price's Chandos House facade.

The drive serpentines to the west front. This front, like the others, is built of unusually lovely stone, quarried on the estate, golden with a silvery mantling of lichen derived from the centuries. It is compact and noble. A temple-like centrepiece of four giant pilasters projects. Over the cornice of the order an attic storey supports a pediment. The influence of Vanbrugh is conspicuous in the massive keystones of the ground floor windows and entrance door.

There is no disturbing discrepancy in the recessed south front, also temple-like, with projecting end wings, which form most useful closets within doors, little writing rooms, retreats and bathrooms, all with tiny fireplaces, mostly set across corners. As for the east front it has a central bow from ground to parapet of five windows on each floor. The effect is clumsy yet fascinating. It presented the architect with internal difficulties which he adroitly resolved with curving walls. Nash's detached greenhouse, composed of a serried row of Ionic columns between glazed openings and end pediments of pretty glass roundels completes the happy ensemble. These three fronts – the fourth, or back of the house is hidden away and, admittedly nondescript – settle themselves into a harmonious whole, the conception of one outstanding designer.

The interior of Barnsley is no less striking than the exterior. From the west front one steps straight into a hall of two storey height and resplendent in decoration. The only English counterpart

The Hall fireplace of stuccowork over marble.

Barnsley Park, the east front and John Nash's conservatory of 1806-1810.

that occurs to me is the hall at Clandon in Surrey, which, although larger, is less lavish – indeed, more stark. Again the names of the stuccoist or stuccoists of the Barnsley hall have not been recorded. Their work however is of the highest craftsmanship. Christopher Hussey of *Country Life* was inclined to attribute the wall panels, the square framed rosettes of the coves and central relief of Diana and Cupid on the flat of the ceiling and the reclining figures of the chimneypiece to Charles Stanley, a Dane, who worked at Hall Place near Maidenhead. All the stucco enrichments are white against a Neapolitan yellow ground. The lock and hinges of the front door, as of most of the doors in the house are of polished brass.

The hall proper fills the centre of the west front. At the far end a screen in two tiers admits through three arched lower openings to an inner hall narrower but of the same height, and decorated with stucco work no less sumptuous. In fact the ceiling wreath which frames a goddess reclining on meringue-like clouds is adorned with plaster fruits and flowers in high relief that vie in delicacy of moulding with Grinling Gibbon's wood carvings. Whoever was Barnsley's architect it is not unreasonable to guess he used that incomparable pair of stuccoists, the Italians Artari and Bagutti, who certainly worked at Cannons. For the work here is really of a very professional standard. Also Rudder's *New History of Gloucestershire* (1779) states categorically that 'The ceilings are done by the best Italian masters.' Geoffrey Beard in his *Georgian Craftsmen* favours Italian workmen chiefly on account of the advanced Baroque patterns used. From the two halls access is given on the north-west to the dining-room, on the south to the drawing-room, on the east to the library, and on the north again to the staircase.

We may assume that Henry Perrot on his marriage to the rich Bourchier heiress got busy decorating the interior of the house which on his father-in-law's death was only a shell and which his future wife, still a child, had naturally enough left untouched. She probably lived with her guardians in Barnsley House in the village, a very attractive Cotswold style house which her father Brereton Bourchier had built in 1697. Until 1984 it was the home of David Verey, the Gloucestershire historian, and is now that of his widow, Rosemary, the well known garden writer. Mrs. Perrot, dying in 1732, predeceased her husband. It is probable that since he instigated the decoration of Barnsley he also completed the stuccowork. On his death in 1740 two spinster daughters reigned at Barnsley Park. In 1778 the survivor Cassandra left the estate to a descendant of her father's sister, James Musgrave, a young man of twenty-seven. He eventually succeeded to a baronetcy and was responsible for the later decorative styles introduced to the house. About 1780 James Musgrave called upon a west country architect, Anthony Keck, to decorate the dining-room. Keck who had done work for

The Library in the Empire style by John Nash. The figures are painted black on a terra cotta ground.

The upstairs Oak Room. The relief in the stucco chimneypiece is supposedly of Catherine Brydges, wife of Brereton Bourchier.

Robert Adam at Moccas Court, Herefordshire and at Flaxley Abbey, Gloucestershire, was a perfectly respectable but unexciting architect whose style was weak Adam-cum-Wyatt. His dining-room at Barnsley, the walls now of Wedgwood blue, has a marble fire-place with fine central plaque of a classical sacrifice. The five-windowed drawing-room on the south front has doors painted to feign maplewood with marginal lines painted or stencilled to resemble ebony. The library on the east front is rendered unusual by the graceful curve of the great window bow. The decoration here by John Nash in the 'Empire' style, of candelabra, gryphons and figures painted black on a terracotta ground, is an appropriate termination to the Baroque exoticism of the other state rooms.

With the front stairs we return to the exquisite stucco decoration by the Italians, only less exuberant than that of the two halls. The ceiling design is in lower relief, and the wall medallions of the Virtues are almost stately. The ground colour of the walls is a paler version of that of the halls, a sort of straw yellow. The veneered stair handrail is elegant; the iron balusters are stalwart. At the top of the stairs a gallery spans the inner hall, enabling us to have a close look at the ceiling and upper wall panels which contain oval bas-reliefs of members of the Perrot family. In the upstairs Oak Room an elaborate stucco chimneypiece of a portrait relief (Mrs. Perrot's mother Catharine Bourchier has been suggested) upheld by cherubs under gathered drapery, is so identical to one at Hall Place, Maidenhead that it led Christopher Hussey to attribute all the plasterwork in the house to Charles Stanley.

In 1875 the Wykeham family came into the property, adding Musgrave to their name and bringing with them Sir Isaac Newton's library, housed at Barnsley until hundreds of books were sold piecemeal in 1920. The remainder were bought seven years later by the Pilgrim Trust and presented to Trinity College, Cambridge. In 1934 the Wykeham-Musgraves sold the property to Lady Violet Henderson, the present Lord Faringdon's grandmother. Until that date it had passed by inheritance since 1548. Lady Violet's son Gavin, 2nd Lord Faringdon, was chiefly responsible for the impressive garden layout in radiating rides of beech hedge interspersed with statuary.

Unlike many of the houses in this volume, which may be cosier, more sympathetic, even more lovable just because they have grown so to speak out of their native soil, Barnsley Park is quite different. Admittedly it looks a foreigner in the Cotswolds; but a very welcome one. It is sheer architecture; it is a concerted work of art. It came about by no accident. You could not slice off a wing, or a fraction of any part of the three fronts without total ruination of the whole, any more than you could knock off a leg or arm of a Chippendale chair or the spout of a silver tea-pot by Lamerie. Apart too from its harmonious design the crispness of every mould and bracket is a triumph of the Georgian stone mason's craftsmanship.

Batsford Park

Top. Batsford Park, the entrance front of the house built for Lord Redesdale between 1888-1892.

Bottom. The garden front.

'On Christmas Day Lord and Lady Redesdale with some young people were playing at Snap Dragon but having unfortunately put the Raisins into the Spirits of Wine instead of Brandy, the Raisins bounced about and three ladies were set in a blaze, two were burnt most dreadfully and were obliged to keep their beds for many days.' Surprisingly enough these bright young people were not friends of the Mitford sisters about whom we read so much today, but an earlier generation. The author of this passage was not Nancy (the adverb *unfortunately* might well make us suppose so) but prim Miss Anne Rushout of neighbouring Northwick Park in her unpublished Journal of 1813.

The Lord Redesdale mentioned was not then Uncle Matthew in *The Pursuit of Love* but Sir John Mitford, who had been made Speaker of the House of Commons 1801-02 in the place of Addington, and Lord Chancellor of Ireland 1802-6. On this appointment Sir John Mitford was created Lord Redesdale. According to the D.N.B. Lord Redesdale's 'integrity was unimpeachable, his manners were stiff, and his sense of humour was deficient.' In 1808 he inherited (not entirely unexpectedly) from a rich and highly respected Gloucestershire squire, Thomas Edwards-Freeman, the Batsford estate of several thousand acres and a pleasant early-Georgian seat. Freeman was the childless husband of Lord Redesdale's mother's sister, and the ostensible reason for the bequest was that he too had an ancestor who had held the office of Lord Chancellor of Ireland under Queen Anne. A supplementary reason was the manner in which Lord Redesdale's son won the testator's heart. One day the father took his little boy to see Mr. Freeman who to amuse the child played for him on a crazy old barrel organ. When the performance was over the child said to his father, 'Give the poor old man a shilling.'

In return for the inheritance of Batsford, Lord Redesdale was obliged to assume by royal licence the additional name and arms of Freeman. Dying in 1830 he was succeeded by his son Thomas as 2nd Lord. Thomas played an active, if not prominent part in the House of Lords, by becoming chairman of innumerable committees. An opponent of reform he held strong religious views, being vociferously opposed to the doctrine of the Real Presence. In 1877 he was made Earl of Redesdale by Disraeli. He never married but lived with a devoted sister at Batsford where he died in 1886. Both the barony and the earldom became extinct.

The Earl was succeeded in his estates by his cousin Algernon Bertram Freeman-Mitford, grandfather of the Mitford sisters, who was made by his great friend King Edward VII in 1902 1st Lord Redesdale of the second creation. Bertram or Bertie (pronounced Bartie) Mitford was cultivated, well-bred and extremely handsome. He moved in exclusive London circles and the Marlborough House set. In 1863 he was sent as second secretary to the Embassy in St. Petersburg. The lure of the East captivated him and in 1886 he managed to get transferred to Tokyo. He learned to speak Japanese and concluded some difficult negotiations with the Mikado. Of his several books published the most famous was *Tales of Old Japan*. From 1874 to 1886 he was appointed Secretary to the Board of Works which brought him into ever closer touch with the Prince of Wales. He also associated with artists like Whistler, Leighton and Millais, and with men of letters like Carlyle and Edmund Gosse.

Bertram Mitford, 1st Lord Redesdale, riding with his daughter Frances and son, Rupert.

This Prince Charming became a great favourite of his lonely old cousin the Earl of Redesdale, who practically treated him as a son. Bertram Mitford recalls in his *Memories* a first idyllic visit to Batsford during the holidays from Eton, chiefly spent in shooting and hunting. Although he deeply loved Batsford he disliked the early Georgian house, and from the moment of his inheritance intended to demolish it. It is curious that in his *Memories* and *Further Memories* he makes no mention of this tremendous operation and the replacement. To judge from old engravings the early Georgian house does not seem to have been out of the ordinary. It was a decent rectangular box of two storys under a balustrade. When his son David, the 2nd Lord Redesdale, as a little boy of eight saw the windows being pulled out of the old house, he burst into tears.

The early-Georgian Batsford Park from an engraving of 1824. It was demolished in 1888.

Between 1888 and 1892 Bertram Mitford built the present house on a different site. The view is a fine one overlooking the Sezincote estate to the right and Moreton-in-the-Marsh town, two miles away, to the left. The style of the new house was entirely different to its predecessor and was dictated by Mitford. It is fundamentally and chastely Elizabethan, on the conventional E plan, with mullioned windows and pointed gables. The architect employed was Sir Ernest George, then in partnership with Harold Peto, better known as a garden landscapist. George, a gifted draftsman with a leaning to the pictorial, was a domestic architect and rival in popularity to Norman Shaw. It was said that as Robert Adam discovered Dalmatia, so Ernest George discovered Holland. The Dutch influence is conspicuously apparent in George's Claridge's Hotel and other London houses, like that for W.S. Gilbert in Collingham Gardens in South Kensington, which fairly bristles with stepped and curvilinear gables. These flamboyances are absent at

Batsford Park, the Hall, two floors in height and of baronial dimensions.

Batsford, thanks no doubt to the owner's sense of what befitted his dignity and status in the English landowning hierarchy. It is significant too that the clerk-of-works who supervised the building was the future Cotswold architect, Sir Guy Dawber. Batsford was the first house in which Dawber played a part and ever afterwards he constructed his own houses in stone with the minimum of elaboration in the detail. Stowell Park and Swinbrook Manor are examples in the neighbourhood.

Indeed Batsford house, in its buff coloured stone quarried from an adjacent field, is uniformly simple and traditional. The entrance front, facing north-west into a hill, has a central projecting porch between two advancing arms. That on the right contains a huge ballroom with oriel window reaching through two storeys on the side elevation; lesser windows are irregularly spaced. The garden front facing south-east consists of eight windows on each floor, broken into three projecting bays, all under pointed gables. A battalion of tall clustered chimney-stacks perforates the sky-line. The house stands on a raised terrace of mown grass, originally guarded by a regiment of Irish yews, with views down to Lord Redesdale's famous garden. A pair of garden pavilions form bastions at either end of the terrace.

The porch leads to a vast hall, its walls of dressed stone with enrichments verging on *art nouveau*. It is a noble, or should I say, a baronial room, two floors in height. From it rises the staircase in long flights to a gallery running the length of the inner wall.

One of the loggias on the south-east front.

Stairs and gallery are of carved oak in a shiny yellow varnish which imparts to the room a nostalgic smell all its own. The ceiling is likewise timbered. A round vaulted passage leads to a garden entrance on the south front. The great ball-room, occupying the right wing of the entrance front has a high raftered roof. The dining-room ceiling was originally composed of cross beams stencilled black and red, of which a section survives in a serving room carved out of it earlier this century. The present plaster ceiling is a copy of a late Elizabethan ceiling of strapwork and pendant pattern. So too is the ceiling of the large drawing-room facing the terrace.

The new Batsford was built at a time of supreme confidence in the future of the English country house. King Edward VII was once or twice entertained by Lord and Lady Redesdale for enormous house parties. Lord Ronald Leveson-Gower, staying there in July 1897 could find nothing more to say than, 'The house is a very roomy and a most comfortable one, of no style in particular, with a large hall and a spacious dining-room. There are some family portraits, but the principal feature of this place is over a mile of wild garden.' It amazed him that Sir Ernest Satow, our Minister in Japan, and the Keeper of Kew Gardens were fellow guests. But Bertram Mitford was more interested in his garden than house. And he created it largely under the influence of Sir Joseph Hooker. He went to limitless lengths to obtain oriental plants and shrubs. In another book *The Bamboo Garden*, his enthusiasm for his subject was allowed to run rampant. So too in the garden, for he planted no less than fifty species at Batsford, brought from the Himalayas, China, Japan and the United States.

The Hon. Iris Mitford in a phaeton at the front door, c. 1900.

Lord Redesdale's extravagance in building and gardening brought about a serious decline in his fortunes. In 1910 he was obliged to let the house. Since Batsford was only completed in 1892 its Victorian glory lasted a mere eighteen years. Lord Redesdale moved his family to London's Pont Street. After his eldest son Clement's death in the Great War he returned for a short twilight period. Even so, a part only of the house was in use; the rest was under dustsheets. When he died in 1916 he was succeeded by his eldest surviving son David who was serving in the Army. The 2nd Lord Redesdale and his wife lived in the big house for a few years with a skeleton staff. The eldest of their growing family, Nancy, Pamela and Tom, were brought up there as small children in a happy and carefree manner. But in 1919 Lord Redesdale sold Batsford to Sir Gilbert Wills, Bt., later created Lord Dulverton. During Lord and Lady Dulverton's reign Batsford enjoyed between the two World Wars an Indian summer of prosperity, entertainment and enjoyment. His son the 2d Lord Dulverton lives in part of the house today. One of the leading foresters in Great Britain, he not only maintains the large gardens and wood but has greatly improved and extended them.

Beverston Castle

Samuel and Nathaniel Buck's engraving of Beverston Castle, 1732.

In the second act of *Richard II*, Bolingbroke meets Northumberland in 'the Wilds of Glostershire'. 'How far is it, my lord, to Berkeley now?' he enquires, to receive Northumberland's answer, 'Believe me, noble lord, I am a stranger here in Glostershire. These high wild hills, and rough uneven ways, Draw out our miles, and make them wearisome.' Beverston, so long and intimately connected with the Berkeley family, and on the direct route to Berkeley Castle from Cirencester and indeed from London, is situated in just such rough, uneven country as Shakespeare described. In the poet's day the flat, high plain was practically devoid of trees and must have been inhospitable indeed.

Beverston Castle is barely glimpsed from the road. You can pass through the village, mostly comprising neat semi-detached cottages by the early-Victorian architect Lewis Vulliamy, before you realise that you have reached it. The romantic approach to the castle is not by its drive but by a lane to the church which runs between two old walls so overhung with spreading beech trees that they form a tunnel of greenery. Once at the church, the north side of the castle frowns overhead, a grim, grey huddle of towers and turrets, only a little more ruinous than they were shown in Samuel and Nathaniel Buck's fine engraving of 1732.

Beverston Castle, bridge over the moat from castle to garden.

Medieval Beverston Castle was a strongly fortified manor house rather than a fortress built for defence; yet there is irony in the fact that whereas it escaped assault in the savage middle ages it was irreparably damaged by Parliamentary forces during the Civil Wars. The land on which the castle stood had been Berkeley property since time immemorial. For some misdemeanour the Berkeleys forfeited it to the Norman Kings. Henry II gave it to Robert FitzHardinge, who settled it on his second son on his marriage to Alice de Gaunt. Their son Maurice, who took his mother's name de Gaunt, was the first builder of the castle in 1225. The property passed through various families by descent, to be bought back in 1350 by Thomas 3rd Lord Berkeley.

The castle was moated all the way round. The Buck brothers' view of 1732 taken from the north-east indicates water encircling it; and a drawing of 1895 taken from the opposite south-west point likewise shows water in front of the two other sides, water spanned

Beverston Castle, the Jacobean wing, 1612-1644.

by a perfectly respectable arched bridge. Today the bridge, if it can be the same one, has assumed the most eccentric shape, rather like a surrealist parabolic curve by the Catalonian architect Gaudí. It is a striking object.

Outside the moat to the east is a courtyard dominated by a venerable walnut tree shown in an early 19th century oil painting by Pieter de Windt. A fellow walnut tree graces the garden. Various dependencies stand round the court including a small but pretty 14th century barn, supported by four buttresses. Below the barn's central gable is a window with an enormous stone lintel, the bevelled ends of which are so lightly poised on the jambs that it is hard to imagine how the weight has been sustained for over six centuries. Within the moat *was* (for on the east side there *is* no longer trace of water) the 14th century detached gatehouse. This picturesque relic consists of an archway and the lower portion of a drum tower. It is a joy to see spring flowers sprouting from the crevices in an abandon which would deeply shock the guardians of state owned monuments with their mania for cement grouting and orderliness. This gatehouse marks the eastern boundary of the inner court, with the great hall of the castle facing it.

Thomas 3rd Lord Berkeley was the possessor who left more mark on the actual castle than any other. He was a sheep breeder on a tremendous scale who bought up surrounding packets of land so as to form a compact estate of colossal acreage. On the

Remains of the Castle's 14th century detached gatehouse.

The medieval castle and Jacobean wing seen across the moat, now dry.

manor estate he sheared in one year as many as 5,775 sheep for the Stroud woollen factories. To Lord Berkeley was committed the care of King Edward II, but owing to the humanity with which he treated the unfortunate monarch he was obliged to surrender his charge to a less compassionate gaoler.

Beverston Castle. Three sedilia with Gothic tracery arches in the Berkeley Chapel.

The stalwart Berkeley Tower at the south-west corner of the castle is Lord Berkeley's work. It contains the two most interesting medieval apartments, namely the Berkeley Chapel and Great Chamber, both approached by an octagonal turret stair. A great chain of indeterminate age encircles the turret to tie it to the tower. The Chapel is on the first floor. The square nave roof has an elaborate criss-cross of ribs with carved bosses. One of a man's head with bristling moustache is a very lively piece of carving. The resemblance to that of a recent Post Office Trades Union secretary is startling. Nave and sanctuary are not well co-ordinated. The latter is at an angle. Its barrel vault with pointed ribs is simpler than the other's. But what makes the sanctuary most remarkable is the three delicate sedilia under Decorated canopies. The Great Chamber is on the floor above the chapel. It has an adjoining oratory, (not directly over the chapel) with a stone slatted squint for persons in the Great Chamber to observe the priest at the altar.

The south wall of the Berkeley Tower facing the garden presents an impressive blank surface of stonework, pierced by two narrow lancet windows with trefoil heads, one above the other; in their simplicity they are about the most elegant windows of the sort I have ever seen. Close to the tower at the west end of the terrace stands a pretty little gazebo on the edge of the moat.

The 3rd Lord Berkeley was succeeded at Beverston by a younger son, and then a grandson, Sir Maurice Berkeley. Sir Maurice was a man of great physical strength and courage who is reputed to have slain a dragon after the beast had devoured innumerable cattle and men. From him the estate descended through several generations until the accession of Sir John Berkeley who squandered most of his lands, save those of Beverston and its castle. His son John, finding himself impoverished by his late father's dissipations sold Beverston in 1597 to Sir John Pointz, thus ending the Berkeley connection. By James I's reign Beverston was in the ownership of Sir Michael Hicks, remaining Hicks-Beach property until 1842 when it was bought by the Holfords to form part of the Westonbirt Estate.

After Sir Michael Hicks died in 1612 his son Sir William, 1st Baronet, extended the medieval castle eastwards by the long narrow Jacobean wing. It was he who witnessed the siege of the royalist castle by the Parliamentarian Colonel Massey in 1644 and its terrible consequences. The stronghold was then commanded by the royalist Colonel Oglethorpe who happened to be more gallant in love than in war. Having stolen forth one night to court a lady in neighbouring Chavenage, to whom he is said to have signalled from the top of the Berkeley Tower, he was pounced upon by Roundhead scouts, captured and taken to Gloucester. The jubilant Colonel Massey hurried there and extracted from the timorous lover information as to the weakest parts of the castle. He instantly returned to Beverston, ordering the raw Lieutenant in charge to surrender, having offered him favourable terms. These being agreed the Lieutenant asked Massey where he intended going next so that he might avoid being there himself. Thus the Royalist strong-hold ignominiously fell, to be 'slighted' by the victorious Roundhead Colonel. Since then the castle has remained a ruin, never to be lived in again.

The 14th century Berkeley Tower with its octagonal staircase turret.

The Jacobean wing, of which the mullion and transom windows date from 1612 to 1644, was burnt some ten years after Sir William Hicks's death in 1680, and rebuilt. It is an attractive range with a large spreading magnolia tree and shrubs adorning it. A rather too narrow doorway gives on to a wide terrace, the eccentric bridge and beautiful garden beyond. The rooms inside, now filled with delightful furniture and paintings, are not in themselves of intrinsic merit, with one exception. At the west end of the Jacobean range, which adjoins the castle, a splendid oak staircase with square newel posts and widely spaced balusters has survived both Colonel Massey's ravages and the fire of 1691. The massive handrail and plain oak treads revive nostalgic memories of seventeenth-century staircases in Oxford colleges, up and down which as an undergraduate one clattered with heavy adolescent footfalls.

Beverston Castle. A late-18th century watercolour by Thomas Hearne.

Under the Holford regime Beverston lapsed into a farmhouse. There is in the church a brass tablet to James Garlick, described as yeoman of Beverston Castle who died in 1911. He has been recorded as 'a typical Gloucestershire farmer, with his hearty greeting and genial hospitality.' In 1939 Beverston was bought by the Hon. Mrs. Arthur Strutt, who with her customary zeal – for she bought and restored a number of derelict manor houses in the district – set about re-converting it into a gentleman's residence and laying out the enchanting garden, with lawns, ancient trees, shrubs and flowers. Her successors Major and Mrs. Laurence Rook, have continued to improve both house and garden, and its present air of spaciousness and comfort makes a striking contrast to the gaunt outline of the castle ruins.

Bourton House

Top. Bourton House, the early-18th century Queen Anne front.

Bottom. The garden front, with projecting wings and steep pitched roof.

Motoring from Moreton-in-the-Marsh on the Worcester road we come after two miles to the foot of a steep ridge. The road, now horribly busy, pushes through the main street of the little village of Bourton-on-the-Hill. On either side pretty stone cottages try to ignore the hurly-burly of traffic, their garden walls cascading clumps of aubretia, arabis or stonecrop on to the narrow pavements. At the very foot of the hill, part of the village and yet detached from it, Bourton House stands a little back from the road and protected from it by a high wall with three massive gateways, now permanently closed. Except the rather ungainly vicarage beside the church it is the only building with a claim to gentility.

In the late 16th century Bourton House was in the ownership of the Overbury family, of which the famous Sir Thomas was a son. His father Sir Nicholas, a judge in Wales and recorder of Gloucester, wrote that Thomas 'was instructed in all those qualities which become a gentleman.' He entered the Middle Temple. He was 'by the entreaty of my Lord Treasurer [Robert Salisbury], preferred to honour, found favour extraordinary, yet hindered in his expectations by some of his enemies, and to shift off discontent, forced to travel.' He made great friends with one of the nastiest rascals in English history, later the cause of his undoing, Robert Carr, later Earl of Somerset, James I's fancy boy.

Were Thomas Overbury's good looks the indirect cause of his troubles? 'When Tom was made server to King James,' his father continued, 'His Maty exclaimed "Looke you, this is my new server;" and Queen Anne answered, "T'is a pretty young fellow."' She had no liking for him and was heard to say, 'There goes Carr and his Governor,' meaning Overbury as his confidant. It was through the influence of Carr that Overbury was knighted and became one of the King's Gentlemen. Sir Thomas was appointed Secretary to the royal favourite. His influence, which was not deleterious, over Carr grew. When Carr made it known that he intended by hook or crook to marry Frances Howard Countess of Essex, his friend endeavoured to dissuade him. Frances accordingly became his avowed enemy. Through her influence Overbury was committed to the Tower in 1613. Carr and Frances put poisonous powders in his food on the pretext that they were good for his health. He died of their ministrations aged 32. His father and mother, Sir Nicholas and Lady Overbury, went up from Bourton to the Tower but were refused permission to see their dying son. Frances and Carr were executed for murder.

Sir Nicholas Overbury sold Bourton to Alexander, the fifth son of Oliver Cromwell's General Sir Francis Popham. A Popham descendant demolished the Tudor house, in which the Overburys had lived, practically to the foundations, and built the present house on the site in the late 17th or early 18th century.

Bourton House. One of the largest barns in the Cotswolds and bearing the date 1570.

Entry to Bourton House today is through an opening which faces one of the largest stone barns in the Cotswolds. It is in excellent state of preservation. It is not medieval and bears the date 1570 and initials R.P. for Richard Palmer, the Elizabethan builder of the house from whom Sir Nicholas Overbury bought it in 1598. At right angles to the barn are the Tudor brewhouse, and the stable block, now converted to a cottage. This delightful complex of buildings allows access to an inner court bounded by the east front of the rectangular house. Great stone piers carrying balls are cut into the end walls of the brewhouse and stable blocks in a way I do not think I have ever seen before. Had this not been done there would not be width enough to allow a coach or waggon to enter the court within which an ancient chestnut tree spreads its brawny arms.

Bourton House. A stone pier and ball, curiously cut into the corner wall of the brewhouse. Its fellow pier on the stable block behaves in the same way.

The wall along the road not only shields the house from the public gaze,but allows its inmates to have an uninterrupted first floor view of open fields and the distant woods of Batsford Park. The entrance or north front is a duplication of the garden or south front. A flight of steps with urn finials and pretty curved railings leads to the front door.

The plan of the house is eminently compact and trim. It is rectangular with single bay projections at each corner. It is best appreciated from the garden side. The severity of elevation is mitigated by the golden stone used. Like the north front the south has a centrepiece of Ionic pilasters supporting a pediment. From behind an unadorned parapet rises a steep pitched roof of stone tiles, perforated by dormer windows, and escorted by stalwart chimney stacks at the corners. Sharp straight lines are the motifs of this geometrical and satisfactory facade.

Unfortunately the south windows have recently had their thick Queen Anne sashbars replaced by thin ones of the late Georgian variety and the number of panes increased. Somehow the Victorian conservatory with spiky iron cresting does not seem out of place. From the garden front a mown lawn stretches to an artificially raised grass terrace, undoubtedly contemporary with the house and a feature commonly introduced in the 17th century to afford views over fields and distant hills.

Both west and east fronts are symmetrical and ingenious. The latter facing the stable yard enables one to understand how the corner projecting bays of all four fronts derived from the original

Bourton House, an end wall of the house, with cramped doors and upper windows, yet still strictly symmetrical.

Elizabethan corner turrets. On this front the Elizabethan bases of the two surviving towers determine the Queen Anne character of this delightful house.

The square paved entrance hall leads to an inner hall and wide staircase with fine turned balusters. When I first knew Bourton House the high staircase window was adorned with painted heraldic devices, one to a pane. They too have recently been done away with. Nearly all the rooms are panelled, and the two between a passage on the south front have lately been thrown into one long drawing-room, of which the panelling is of pine, painted yellow. A recent owner substituted for the simple contemporary marble fireplaces a pair of Rococo chimneypieces which do not marry well with the unpretentious wainscot of the walls.

In 1851 the place was bought by Sir James Buller East, Baronet, who bequeathed it to his first cousin (Mrs) Emily Matilda Bligh. She was mother of the owner I knew, Miss Ada Theodosia Bligh, during the last War. She was living here with her old sister, another Miss Bligh. Both the old ladies were very sweet and both wore red wigs. One day I called to inspect the collection of musical instruments from the National Trust's Old Devonshire House in Bloomsbury which the sisters were storing for safety throughout the war. It was as well they did so for the Charles II house from which the instruments came was totally wiped off the map by a bomb. I was given a sumptuous tea. Together we prepared scones in the kitchen which we ate in the dining-room, the old ladies running to and fro like pink mice. They absolutely refused my request that we should eat in the kitchen. Servantless they lived entirely alone in the house.

When the Miss Blighs were living at Bourton the inside of the house was almost unchanged since it had been built. None of the panelling was painted, but left grey and dark in the natural wood. All the rooms were chock-a-block with *bibelots* and the walls heavy with Bligh portraits, for the sisters were descended from the Earls of Darnley.

Since their deaths and the break-up of the property soon after the War the house has fallen into the hands of *eight* different owners. The consequences have been inevitable. Each new owner undid what the last owner did, each redecorating according to his and her taste. The last time I was here some years ago the house had already been tarted up like an old bedizened woman. The hall panelling was painted sealing-wax red; every room had fitted carpets; the lamp-shades were from a smart Mayfair decorator. The house had temporarily lost its soul.

Rapid changes of ownership are happening in many old Cotswold manor houses today, often greatly to the detriment of their character and ambience. Yet Bourton has fallen on its feet, and its present owners, Mr. and Mrs. Richard Paice, are slowly putting the place to rights.

Chastleton House

Chastleton is still in Oxfordshire. I say *still* because it is a miracle that some Whitehall department with a mania for straightening out the counties has not sliced off this Oxfordshire thumb for the crime of sticking into the east flank of its neighbour, Gloucestershire. Chastleton lies within the thumb, and – happily – it lies definitely within the Cotswolds.

Chastleton House, the front of the house taken from an engraving in John Skelton's *The Antiquities of Oxfordshire*, 1823.

In 1602 the estate was bought by Walter Jones from the unfortunate Robert Catesby, who three years later was to lose his life over implication in the Gunpowder Plot. Catesby was in need of funds, 'probably for the purpose of carrying on his vile machinations,' as Skelton wrote in *The Antiquities of Oxfordshire* (1823). At all events he was in no hurry to leave for he did not quit the place until 1605. Now although Walter Jones was a Witney wool stapler he did not consider himself either a merchant or a yeoman. On the contrary he considered himself an esquire. Moreover he proudly traced his lineage back through Brutus King of Britain to Priam King of Troy when Zeus from Mount Olympus directed the armies of the Greeks and Trojans on the plains of Ilium. He was married to Eleanor Pope, daughter of a small county landowner, who had been jeweller to Queen Elizabeth I.

The best way to approach Chastleton is down a lane off the Stow to Great Rollright road. Round a corner in a tract of uneventful pasture land, you are forewarned by a pretty gabled dovecote with cupola and then by an arched gateway with pediment, to expect a gentleman's dwelling. You are not disappointed. Suddenly you are confronted with a high, compact, symmetrical manor house of such dignity and benignity that you gasp. The south front so engrosses you that for a time you ignore the church nestling, in that true English fashion, to one side, in this case dwarfed by the secular mass, plus a stable, brewhouse and bakery block, lying low on the other side of the forecourt. The vertical emphasis of the front is very striking. Mark Girouard has likened the group of five advancing and receding planes under sharp little gables, flanked by a pair of square embattled tower-like structures (to accommodate staircases) to 'a row of jets of water shot up suddenly and poised for the split second before they collapse.' The effect is made dramatic by the disparate but matching windows and the

The Jacobean dovecote.

Chastleton House, the front of the house completed in 1609.

central steps leading to no visible entrance. Girouard sees in the massing of Chastleton the hand of the elusive Tudor-Jacobean architect Robert Smythson, comparing the house with Hardwick Hall in Derbyshire. Another comparable feature is the straight roofline, another the paucity of exterior ornament, which noticeably 'gives it an air of calm composure which no passionate tears or immoderate laughter can disturb.' What is splendid about Chastleton is the way the masses dissolve and regroup themselves in strong lights and sharp shadows as one walks around the house; of which none of the four sides is exactly like its opposite. Whoever did design Chastleton it is architecturally a departure from what was normal in early Jacobean times. The house was all but completed in 1609. Unlike Hardwick Hall, Derbyshire, and Montacute in Somerset, in plan it is compact, not spread; and unlike those great rectangular houses more glass than wall, Chastleton has comparatively small windows and an inner courtyard allowing light to penetrate the rooms from two sides.

Chastleton was nevertheless planned on the old-fashioned great hall and screens passage lines. Instead however of entering the latter from an axially placed front door, the visitor turns left at the top of the external steps to the central recess and passes through a side door in the left bay. The entrance has a Renaissance portal with plume-like cresting and pair of obelisks. By this ingenious, but not unique, device the hall is not entered direct from outdoors.

Through draughts are thus avoided. The narrow screens passage is lit by one of the large ground floor windows; the hall itself by the other. Immediately to the west of the passage is a winter parlour, the offices being reached from the far end. The screen seen from the hall is of oak with elaborate strapwork cresting. Carved figures sprawl on either side of the two openings. Over a plain stone fireplace Walter Jones's portrait hangs in the place of honour between suits of armour, helmets and crossed swords. These objects are exactly as depicted in Joseph Nash's 1840 illustration in *The English Mansions of the Olden Time*. In fact everything seems the same as in the picture, including the panelling, with frieze of dragons, the long oak table, and even the oak arm chair that belonged to Archbishop Laud. The only difference is that Nash shows glazing in the blank windows on either side of the fireplace. On Walter Jones's left hangs his wife Eleanor Pope and on his right their elder son Henry; on Henry's right his wife Anne Fettiplace. The beautiful ring conspicuous on the finger of Eleanor used to be worn by the late Mrs. Whitmore Jones who on showing visitors round the house would display it on her own finger. The massive watch seen in Anne Fettiplace's portrait is still owned by the family. At the dais end of the hall a stag's mounted antlers project from its body which is painted on the wall. Beyond the dais are the Little Parlour, with contemporary panelling painted white, and in the north-east corner the Great Parlour used as the dining-room.

Above the hall and reached by the main staircase in the west embattled tower, an amazing staircase round a square well encaged by tiers of waisted balusters in carved wood, and newel posts of pierced obelisks, is the Great Chamber. This richly decorated room was likewise illustrated by Joseph Nash, who always added figures dressed in what he believed to be the correct costumes of the

Top left. Chastleton House, the Great Hall, taken from Joseph Nash's *The English Mansions of the Olden Times*, 1840.

Above. The Great Hall, looking from the screens to the dais end, with stag over the door.

Below. The main staircase with newel posts of pierced finials.

ancient time. Whereas the hall was meant for everyday use the great chamber was meant for ceremonial. The chimneypiece is a grand affair bearing columns and a coat of arms with mantling; the walls are panelled in elaborate patterns; and in the frieze are small square portrait heads of sibyls and prophets. The ceiling consists of flat ornamented plaster ribs with pendants. Pevsner's volume on Oxfordshire is very censorious of this room. 'Blatantly *nouveau riche*,' he calls it, 'even barbaric, uninhibited by any considerations of insipid good taste.' But then Walter Jones, descended from King Priam though he may have been, was *nouveau riche*. Nevertheless having made a great deal of money he lavished it, as all his peers did not do, upon only one room of state in a large house of which he left the other apartments grave and sombre.

When Walter Jones died in 1632 an inventory of the contents of the house was taken. Several objects mentioned in it are still in place, underlining the sense of continuity that makes the house so remarkable and gives it a feeling of having somehow defied time.

By 1651 Walter's grandson Arthur Jones was living quietly at Chastleton. The political climate was uncertain. The Joneses were royalist to a man. Suddenly the young King Charles II made a bid for his crown. Arthur left his home and rode post-haste to Worcester, only to be a participant in the devastating royal defeat on September 3rd. Meanwhile Arthur's faithful wife Sarah anxiously awaited her husband's return. Sure enough in the middle of the night she heard the sound of his exhausted horse's hooves in the stable-yard. A few minutes later Arthur, worn out and miserable, made his

The Great Chamber on the first floor, the most elaborate room in the house.

appearance. Sarah took him upstairs to their bedroom. While they were eating, her quick ears caught the sound of strangers outside. Instantly she slipped him into a secret closet behind the panelling. She went down to meet a troop of Roundhead horsemen angrily demanding admittance in search of her husband. They had seen Arthur's reeking horse in the stables. They searched every nook and cranny of the house, prodding curtains, tapestries and mattresses with their swords. When they reached the Jones's sleeping chamber they grew suspicious and refused to move. In anger and disappointment they announced that they would stay the night, demanding a meal. This Sarah with the help of her maids provided as quickly as she could. She also supplied copious flagons of wine into which she poured laudanum from her medicine chest. In due course the soldiers fell into profound stupour. She then opened the door of the closet, led her husband over the prostrate bodies of the soldiers, chose the freshest of the Roundheads' horses and despatched him to safety. When the Roundheads woke up and learnt how they had been duped their rage was great. At first Sarah, her children and Arthur's old father Henry who was living in the house feared for their lives. But they were left unharmed. Moreover beyond a small fine there was no molestation of Arthur who returned home after two years to resume a discreet domestic life at Chastleton throughout the remaining term of the Commonwealth. We can imagine the rejoicing when King Charles II was restored to the throne of his ancestors in 1660. The Joneses, like so many Tory gentry remained faithful to the Stuarts, becoming Jacobites as well as Cavaliers.

Sarah Jones, who hid her husband Arthur from Cromwellian soldiers after the Battle of Worcester in 1651.

When the last male Jones died without children in 1828 he left Chastleton to descendants of his grandmother Whitmore's family from Dudmaston in Shropshire. They tacked Jones to their own name. In the second half of the last century three Whitmore-Jones brothers and a sister succeeded one another. From them the estate passed to the late Alan Clutton-Brock, art correspondent of *The Times* and Slade Professor of Fine Art, whose widow lives there today, as distinguished a part of the house's history as any Mistress Jones before her.

It is not exaggerating to affirm that there is no room in Chastleton which does not evoke the past, whether the Needlework Room, its walls hung with flaming stitch, sometimes known as Hungarian work, the Fettiplace Room with its tapestries, couch work bed-cover of Queen Anne date, oak fireplaces and panelling painted a faded mustard, or the Library, abounding in ancient tomes, including a first edition of the *Eikon Basilike* and the Bible used by Charles on the scaffold and handed to Bishop Juxon with the mystical word, 'Remember'. The Juxon family house was at Long Compton two miles away. The Bishop would hold Church of England services in Chastleton's great hall when their celebration was forbidden by law during the Commonwealth.

Chastleton House, the Long Gallery, running the whole length of the north front.

The circle of yews, originally cut in the shape of animals and birds etc.

Finally on the top floor the Long Gallery runs the whole length of the north front. If this apartment were the only one of interest in the house it would justify Chastleton's preservation for all time, for it is one of the most glorious rooms in England. It is long and low with a wide barrel ceiling, plastered from end to end with an intricate interlaced pattern in relief, which is the very opposite of oppressive. The stuccoists were probably Oxford men. The Long Gallery is lit by ample windows. From the eastern window one looks down upon a topiary garden of indeterminate age. Within a circle of yews are twenty-four box trees, formerly cut in the shape of animals, birds, toads, even a female elephant with her young, a crown, a ship, rings and globes, which in their prime were, to be honest, more curious than beautiful. Today, as Mrs. Clutton-Brock observes, they rather resemble Henry Moore figures, and as such are an aesthetic improvement. From the other windows of the gallery there is nothing unsightly. Lawns, trees, meadows and greenery seem to embrace the rich blood orange walls.

I know no country house of this date, not even Cranborne Manor in Dorset, that gives me the feeling of arrested time, that rare feeling which I used to experience in Spanish churches and cathedrals, of the remote past literally encompassing me. Chastleton is the sleeping beauty of English country houses *par excellence*.

Chavenage

Top. Chavenage. The entrance front rebuilt by Edward Stephens in 1576. From an engraving by J. and H. S. Storer of 1827.

Bottom. The south front. The Chapel is just visible on the left.

Storer and Brewer in *Delineations of Gloucestershire* (1825) made a curious reference to the rash of industrial works which had lately developed in the surroundings of Chavenage. 'The poetical and pictorial *visiter*,' they wrote, 'will perhaps regret that scenes so congenial to their tastes are not left in the dignity of solitude, or, at most, free from any other interruption than the venerable manor-house, or rural tenement, fraught with tales of the *olden time*, or wearing the semblance of peace and simplicity.' Having warned the reader what to expect, satanic mills, belching chimneys, pits, waste and blackness, they then adopted the democratic tone. 'The civil economist, however, less pleasing but more useful in his views and considerations, will be gratified to find that the rivulets which steal through these sweet vales, are made conducive to the employment of a busy population, engaged in the clothing manufacture.' These words were written exactly 160 years ago. Well, all I can say is that one *visiter* of 1987, admittedly not at all 'useful in his views and considerations', being no economist, finds nothing of the sort. The two mile lane from Tetbury town passes through totally unspoilt flattish Cotswold uplands, with no sign of a working mill or busy population. In fact on reaching Chavenage he feels he may be a million miles from teeming industry.

Chavenage was once the property of that ubiquitous and featureless sister of Edward the Confessor, Princess Goda. Since she has no entry in the *Dictionary of National Biography* there is nothing to say about her. By the second year of William the Conqueror's reign Chavenage was the property of the monks of Horsley Abbey, some five miles away to the north-west. At the Dissolution it was granted by King Henry VIII to Edward Seymour, the future Lord Protector. But it soon changed hands and in 1564 was bought by the Stephens family, wealthy landowners from Eastington and Lypiatt and sheep farmers on an extensive scale. Edward Stephens virtually built the present house in 1576, carefully leaving his and his wife's initials and the date on the labels of the moulding over the front door.

There was a smaller house on the site. Stephens totally transformed whatever was there before, adding the projecting wings and central porch, thus fashioning the entrance front into so perfect an E that one wonders whether the dearly cherished tradition, now spurned by the architectural historians, that it was done in honour of the Virgin Queen, is not correct. Certainly this front is seen in its fully glory as one turns between a splendid pair of stone gate piers, crowned by exceptionally lovely Queen Anne urns, into a short drive. Sloping lawns on either side and overhanging cedar trees form a sort of mount to the picture. It is a breath-taking spectacle with a pair of prodigiously high windows reaching from the very ground up to the eaves. The texture of the stone used – it is extraordinary how Cotswold stone varies – is of a dusky, mauvey-grey hue, part ashlar and part rubble. The stone-tiled roof is steep, a glorious plane of moss and lichen, interrupted only by two little dormers and one tall chimney stack which rises from the porch. Some of the stone used is said to have come from Horsley Priory which was in ruins when Edward Stephens got busy. Almost certainly his descendant, Colonel Nathaniel, in widening the south projecting arm in the 1630's, brought from Horsley Priory odd pieces of 14th- century masonry which he inserted here and there.

Chavenage. The Great Hall.

This Nathaniel Stephens made quite a figure in the Civil War. Soldier and lawyer he was M.P. for Gloucestershire when the troubles broke into armed conflict. A moderate Parliamentarian he avowed himself an adherent of Oliver Cromwell, to whom he was related. Yet during the siege of royalist Beverston Castle less than two miles away, the Colonel took no part against his neighbour. The truth is he was inclined to sit on the fence.

While Colonel Nathaniel was celebrating Christmas of 1648 he was showing such irresolution over the decision to do King Charles I to death that Oliver Cromwell himself, accompanied by his son-in-law General Henry Ireton came down to Chavenage 'to whet his almost blunted purpose.' The self-invited guests are said to have sat up all night before extracting their host's reluctant acquiescence to become a regicide. Cromwell and Ireton may have gone away satisfied, but Nathaniel's family were horrified. His old father and daughter Abigail strongly upraided him for yielding to his guests' wicked importunities. Less than three months after the King's execution on January 30th 1649 the Colonel fell ill. On the 2nd May he died, expressing with his last breath regret for having participated in his Sovereign's execution.

The Tapestry Room in which Oliver Cromwell slept in 1648. The Flemish tapestries depict the adventures of Don Quixote.

Timbs and Gunn's *Abbeys, Castles and Ancient Halls* of 1872 records the legend that when all the Stephens relations were assembled at Chavenage for the Colonel's funeral,

'and their several well known equipages were crowding the courtyard to proceed to the churchyard, the household were surprised to observe that another coach, ornamented with even more than the gorgeous embellishments of that splendid period, and drawn by black horses, was approaching the porch in great solemnity. When it arrived the door of the vehicle opened in some unseen manner; and, clad in his shroud, the shade of the lord of the manor glided into the carriage, and the door instantly closing upon him, the coach rapidly withdrew from the house; not

The Great Hall chimneypiece.

A panel in the Oak Room, depicting one of the four Muses.

however with such speed but there was time to perceive that the driver was a beheaded man, that he was arrayed in the royal vestments, with the Garter moreover on his leg, and the star of that illustrious order on his breast. No sooner had the coach arrived at the gateway of the manor court, than the whole appearance vanished in flames of fire. The story further maintains that, to this day, every lord of Chavenage dying in the manor house takes his departure in this awful manner.'

On my visit to Chavenage I did not like to ask the present owner whether the practice was fulfilled on the demise of his predecessor.

Entering the house by the porch below the beautiful gothic Decorated window (presumably another importation from Horsley Priory, for a plain Tudor window is shown in an engraving of 1807) you find yourself in the screens passage, with the great hall on your left. The hall, two storeys in height, and with a flat plaster ceiling, is lit by those two stupendous windows we admired from outside. They are partly filled with fragments of glass panels, some of which seem too profane to have come from the Priory. The lower part of the screen under which we passed is Elizabethan, the upper part which bears a minstrels' gallery and organ having been tampered with. The chimneypiece, rather like a Jacobean monument with large central medallion of black touchstone encircled by a wreath of bay-leaves, bears the arms of the builder, Edward Stephens's son. Whereas during the Stephens's long tenure walls were hung with Civil War armour, 'Indian snowshoes and other curiosities', today their place has been taken by pictures of the Lowsley-Williams family.

Up the main staircase three bedrooms with historic names are shown. Those of Ireton and Cromwell adjoin. The latter is hung with early 17th-century Flemish tapestry depicting the Adventures of Don Quixote (a subject one does not readily associate with the staid Lord Protector), and remarkably well preserved. When the tapestry was recently cleaned a copy of *The Railway Times* of 1840 was found behind it, indicating when it was last taken down for the same purpose. Queen Anne's Room recalls a royal visit, and the bedroom was also occupied by Princess Marie Louise, a granddaughter of Queen Victoria, when she was writing her book, *My Memories of Six Reigns*. The credulous princess claimed that the ghost of a renegade royalist officer repeatedly opened her bedroom door at night and that her maid in an adjoining room saw the ghost of a grey lady.

The panelling of the downstairs Oak Room is wainscoted with unusual late Elizabethan or Jacobean panelling. Corinthian pilasters carved with strapwork device and frieze with geometrical pattern are parti-gilt. Four remarkable panels, known as the Four Muses below the Tree of Life (although one Muse has a pointed beard) are contemporary. They have been re-set within an alcove dating from Edwardian times.

Indeed at the rear of the house a whole Edwardian wing has been tacked on. Built of the same stone as the original house and in the same style it blends well on the outside, although the great ballroom it contains is cumbersome. Beyond the ballroom, and attached to the west side of the house by a narrow passage is the Chapel with a high tower like that of a parish church. It is an 18th-century folly. Its windows are made up of bits and pieces (more spoils from Horsley Priory?) and it has carved figures of children taken from a Jacobean tomb let into the walls of the porch. A robed monk is said to haunt the Chapel. Two people claim to have encountered him since the last war. The Chapel contains a memorial to George Williams Lowsley Hoole-Lowsley-Williams who died in 1937, whose many names are an amusing example of the absurdities the English landed gentry were obliged to put up with from the College of Heralds on inheriting property in late Victorian times.

The Stephens family, once so prosperous and the possessors of large estates through the breeding of Cotswold sheep, became less and less affluent. In the last century they ceased to live at Chavenage, which they let and mortgaged to the rich Holfords of Westonbirt. Finally in 1891 the great-grandfather of the present owner bought Chavenage from the last Stephens representative.

With four generations of Lowsley-Williams Chavenage has acquired a character all its own and amassed a fascinating collection of family treasures. One of the pleasures of a visit to this house is the casual things of sentimental and local interest to be encountered on almost every table and shelf. Among them the Chavenage Cricket Book of 1880, with match scores totalling 8 against 0; several nephews of the great W.G. Grace were among the players. Albums of cartes-de-visites of great-great uncles and aunts in studied poses. Records of the Australian Flying Corps in the Great War and an American Topographical Battalion in the Second World War. An invitation to attend the Coronation of 1911 to Major Lowsley-Williams's grandfather who was High Sheriff that year, plus chairs and Coronation medals. Then there is a nearly complete collection of Civil War horse furniture, a leather hat cover and some weapons – all of which makes Chavenage so much a family house and adds to its character.

Chavenage. The Chapel from the west.

Cirencester House

Cirencester, in my youth pronounced Ciceter, sometimes Cicester and occasionally Ciren for short, but *never* Cirencester, which I still have to think twice before enunciating, is generally known as the Capital of the Cotswolds. One of the two most important cities of Roman Britain it was the junction of the Fosse Way, Ermin Way and Akeman Street. The Emperor Constantine is supposed to have been crowned there and in the Dark Ages it became the frontier fort of the West Saxons against the Mercians during the Heptarchy. In 1117 St Mary's Abbey was founded, the Augustinian monks of which made Cirencester into one of the largest English wool staples. At the Dissolution all the surrounding monastic lands were split into two tythings, the western Tything of Oakley being finally purchased in 1695 by Sir Benjamin Bathurst, member of an ancient and wealthy family from Sussex.

Allen, 1st Lord Bathurst by Kneller.

Sir Benjamin, son of George Bathurst, was the youngest of thirteen brothers, six of whom had lost their lives fighting for King Charles I in the Civil War. He became a Governor of the East India Company. Through his marriage to a daughter of Sir Allen Apsley, a royalist in high favour at court, he was made Falconer to King Charles II, became Treasurer of the Household of Princess Anne and, on her succession to the throne, her Cofferer. He died in 1704 having already made over the Cirencester property to his eldest son Allen.

Allen Bathurst was a young man of twenty who at the age of eight had been contracted 'in jest to please his grandmother,' Lady Apsley, to marry his first cousin, Catherine Apsley, aged four. On the death of Sir Benjamin the marriage was re-enacted and for 76 years the couple remained man and wife. Before he came of age Allen was elected M.P. for Cirencester. Politically unambitious he was nevertheless a stalwart Tory, an adherent to the Stuart cause and the champion of his two friends, the statesmen, Henry St. John and Robert Harley. In 1712 he was one of a dozen Tories raised to the peerage to swamp the Upper House and induce the Lords to endorse the Treaty of Utrecht. On Queen Anne's death in 1714 the Tories were discredited and Baron Bathurst retired from active politics.

He did not mind in the least. He was delighted to live the greater part of the year in the country. The first thing he did was to demolish the handsome Jacobean house called Oakley Grove, which had been raised by the Danvers family, and rebuild it; the second to create a park according to the latest notions of taste and fashion. The house he built was in many respects as conservative as his politics. To begin with, he did not, as was the Whig custom, choose a site away from the town. On the contrary he kept the rectangular foundations of the Danvers centre block, having obliterated the two east-projecting wings. He merely distanced his new house from Cirencester town by a three-quarter circle of high yew hedge in the manner of Bernini's colonnade before St. Peter's on an infinitely smaller scale. The hedge is pierced by three green arches, the central leading to an imposing entrance gateway of rusticated and frostwork stone. Cirencester House, as it is now called, of two plain fronts without orders, their single ornamental feature being a small pointed pediment on the east and a segmental one on the west, can hardly be termed a gem of architecture. Almost certainly Lord Bathurst was his own architect. There are no references amongst the family papers even to the names of local masons employed. In short, Bathurst was fairly indifferent to the appearance of his country seat. 'I think any house good enough to sleep in,' he said airily; and to Alexander Pope he remarked when the work was finished in 1718, 'I trust you to give an account how it comes to be so oddly bad.'

Top. Cirencester House from the church tower.

Bottom left. The entrance front facing the town. The 1st Earl Bathurst may have been his own architect in 1712-18.

Bottom right. The front facing the park. The extension to the left was added by Sir Robert Smirke, c. 1820.

The long east front was built of solid ashlar. But the whole of the ground floor was brought forward to give much needed depth to the rooms behind and a portico added in about 1820 for the 3rd Earl Bathurst by Sir Robert Smirke, the Greek Revivalist architect of the British Museum. Some ten years previously Smirke had added a service block to the north end. A later Victorian hand rendered the west front in stucco and substituted plate glass for sash windows.

The principal rooms of the house were consequently much altered and redecorated, albeit conservatively, by Smirke. The narrow rectangular hall with sweeping staircase and balustraded gallery is his. At the turn of this century it was much messed about and has lately been restored to its neo-Greek chastity by the present Earl Bathurst greatly to its improvement. The impressive Roman marble columns, carrying busts, were procured in Italy in 1814 by Lord Apsley, son and heir of the 3rd Earl, who having been Secretary of State for War throughout Wellington's campaigns was attending the Congress of Vienna. Indeed the huge and splendid equestrian portrait of the Great Duke mounted on his charger, Copenhagen, and painted by Lawrence in 1817, was given to the 3rd Earl by the sitter. An accompanying painting of the Battle of Waterloo, dated 1825, was likewise a gift by the Duke, as a note in his handwriting records.

The Duke of Wellington on Copenhagen, given to the 3rd Earl.

The dining-room to the right of the front door was enlarged by

The Hexagon, built by the 1st Earl, to the north of the Broad Avenue.

Smirke. It is of interesting Stuart portraits, probably collected by Sir Benjamin Bathurst, and contains a fine marble chimneypiece, certainly in the Adam style and possibly by Robert Adam himself, who built the original Apsley House at Hyde Park Corner. For when the British Government bought Apsley House from the 3rd Earl to present to the Duke of Wellington in 1816 many of the original fittings were removed. Another, even finer chimneypiece of the same provenance is to be seen in the drawing-room on the west front; and throughout the house are several fine Adam pieces of furniture in mirrors and pier tables. The long library, at the north end of the west front, is hung with an unusual paper imitating Spanish leather. It may well be contemporary with Smirke's alterations. Over the fireplace is a spirited full-length portrait of Lucy St. John, wife of Sir Allen Apsley and grandmother of George Bathurst's wife. Her young son in stiff Jacobean robes stands beside her.

Interesting though the house and contents are the park is undoubtedly the major achievement of the 1st Earl Bathurst, who laid it out with the advice and collaboration of his literary friends, of whom the most intimate was Alexander Pope. The poet's classical learning and vision, and the Earl's taste and practical experience of forestry combined to produce the largest area of Early Georgian landscape layout to survive in Britain.

Pope was devoted to the young, handsome and genial lord, who enjoyed all the fun life had to offer.

'Oh teach us Bathurst Yet unspoiled by wealth!
That secret rare, between the extremes to move
Of mad good nature, and of mean self-love.'

he declaimated in Epistle III of the *Moral Essays*, dedicated to the Earl. He hero-worshipped him. 'I never leave you,' he addressed him in 1735, 'but I wish to say a hundred things to you, and when you go away for any time, I feel my sense of the loss of you tenfold, as men do the loss of life, when it nears it end, though they never know how to make a right use, or possess a full enjoyment of it. You cannot know how much I love you and how gratefully I recollect all the good and obligation I owe to you for so many years.'

Bathurst returned Pope's affection and bore his reproaches ('Batty' was an unpredictable, impetuous, unpunctual gadabout, not to be depended on) with wry amusement. When the poet died in 1744 he left his patron three grisaille oil paintings by Kneller which until lately hung in the hall. He was not the only famous author whom Bathurst befriended. Congreve, Swift, Prior, Gay, Francis Atterbury (Bishop of Rochester) and Sterne were either correspondents or visitors and usually both.

When Bathurst began to plant he was thirty years old. He lived another sixty years, almost but not quite to complete the park. It may be that he felt impelled to rival Badminton in the length of

King Alfred's Hall. The upper photograph shows the Gothic folly as it is today, the engraving a detail of it as it was when finished, c. 1732. A learned antiquarian mistook it for King Arthur's residence.

his rides. He was obliged to buy up additional lands to the west of those manors presented to him by his father. Among them was the Sapperton Estate, including the manor house, like the old Oakley Grove, a splendid Jacobean building which he also demolished. It was left to his son, the 2nd Earl and Lord Chancellor, to extend the Broad Avenue, focussed, oddly enough on Cirencester church tower, to its full five mile limit.

As well as planting trees and laying out avenues (in 1741 when in serious financial straits he focussed the Elm Avenue on the west front of the house, terminating it in a vast Doric column with a statue of Queen Anne on the top) Bathurst littered his landscape with temples and follies. There is little doubt that he designed these himself. They consist of Pope's Seat, a Doric temple flanked by niches, facing south across Seven Rides *rond-point* down an avenue centred on Kemble church; the Hexagon, a handsome affair of arched openings to the north of the Broad Avenue; the Horseguards, a pair of gargantuan sentry boxes at Ten Rides *rond-point*, the crenellated Square Tower, the Round House, Ivy Lodge, a delicious fantasy, half farmhouse, half farm buildings, and King Alfred's Hall. This famous folly, called successively The Hermitage in the Wood, King Arthur's Castle and finally King Alfred's Hall, was begun in 1721 and completed eleven years later after reams of correspondence with Atterbury, Swift and Pope as to its progress and ultimate style. Built of hewn stone and fragments from Sapperton Manor it is the ancestor of all the Gothic follies in Georgian parkscapes. It was immensely admired by the Earl's friends and visitors, Mrs Delany declaring that the building had been mistaken by one learned archaeologist as undoubtedly a residence of King Arthur. Draped in ivy and enclosed by a grove of melancholy yews its setting is still romantic. It was used for *al fresco* meals on summer evenings, and was also the scene of an annual music meeting where the country people assembled to pass the time in fiddling, dancing and drinking.

To within a month of his death at the age of 91 the 1st Earl Bathurst rode two hours a day round his park and drank, without fail, his bottle of claret or madeira after dinner. His son, the straight-laced Lord Chancellor, disapproved of this harmless addiction. But the man who once said that the four most desirable things in life were 'old wood to burn, old wine to drink, old friends to converse with, and old books to read,' paid him no heed whatever. On the contrary one of the last glimpses we get of the sympathetic old Earl comes through a dinner guest at Cirencester when his host was already a nonagenarian. The meal over, the abstemious son withdrew from the table, whereupon the father cried jubilantly, 'Come, now the old gentleman's gone, let us crack another bottle!'

Cold Ashton Manor

Cold Ashton Manor, the entrance porch.

'It is so called from the ash trees growing there,' wrote Sir Robert Atkyns in 1712. That may well be, but the adjective needs no explaining. The place stands 700ft high on the most southerly ridge of the Cotswolds. No position could be more exposed; and there is a legend that during the William Bathursts' ownership in the 1950's, a husband and wife, staying as guests one January, and lacking sufficient bed blankets, crept downstairs to strip the grand piano of its leather covering and again later to drag from under the instrument's legs the carpet on which it stood. Yet dawn would have brought a fitting reward, for the view from the manor house down to St Catherine's Valley and the hills beyond Bath is unsurpassed. There is hardly a building to be seen for miles and the enveloping folds of coombes, hedgerows, woods and fields conceal whatever habitations there may be between house and horizon.

Cold Ashton manor was the property of Bath Abbey until the Dissolution when it was bought by Sir Walter Denys. He made a quick profit by selling it to William Pepwall, an alderman of Bristol who had been Mayor in the 1570's. Pepwall's trade is unknown. He did not survive long and in 1574 left the property to his wife, who may have bought it jointly with William in the first instance. Widow Pepwall, a woman of character, carried on her late husband's unspecified trade. She has been credited with building the present house but stylistic evidence makes this unlikely. The mullions of all the surviving windows are of the ovolo mould which was not common in Tudor times. In any event William Pepwalls' grandson, also christened William, disposed of the estate to a bright apprentice of old Mrs. Pepwall in 1629. This enterprising young man was called John Gunning, an ancestor of the beautiful 18th century Gunning sisters, Lady Coventry and the Duchess of Hamilton, the first of whom died prematurely from clogged pores owing to too much make-up. John Gunning, later a Sheriff and who founded a dynasty, is likely to have been the builder of the existing house. And it was under his roof that the gallant Cornishman, Sir Beville Grenville, was brought to die after the Battle of Lansdown Hill in July 1643. This sympathetic Cavalier was possessed of every good quality but comon sense. He engagingly admitted as much in a sort of writtten apologia:

Top. Cold Ashton Manor, the south front, overlooking St Catherine's Valley and dating from Charles I's reign.

Bottom. The west end, with its harled walls.

I was left to my own little discretion when I was a youth in Oxford, and so fell upon the sweet delights of reading poetry and history in such sort as I troubled no other books, and do find myself so infinitely defective by it, when I come to manage any occasions of weight, as I would give a limb it were otherwise.'

In short, he was hopelessly unpractical. He hastened unprepared to fight for King Charles I with a handful of Cornishmen, barely armed and, as a contemporary wrote, 'so destitute of provisions that the best officers had but a biscuit a day.' Naturally on the field of battle they did not have a chance and their leader was pole-axed.

Like Daneway House and Owlpen Manor Cold Ashton Manor is, or rather was until lately, approached from a lane by some segmental steps to an impressive gateway, too narrow for vehicles. A stone mounting block beside it indicated that you were expected to take horse or tie up at this spot. The gateway cannot be Elizabethan but could well be Jacobean, for the rusticated arch, blocked pilasters, and classical cornice and frieze, correspond with the sort of work Inigo Jones was introducing to England in the second and third decades of the 17th century. Only the diamond panels of the two plinths suggest pre-Inigo Jones provenance. Even so country builders were often well behind the times when it came to interpreting new styles. The carved urns piled high with fruits which flank an elaborate display of the Gunning arms (granted in 1662) must be post-Restoration additions. Unfortunately the central cresting was broken off a long time ago. When the wooden doors, modern replacements of the original ones of unvarnished grey oak, are open, a walled forecourt is disclosed. Ahead is the house, little if at all altered since it was built.

The plan is absolutely symmetrical – a recessed centre with two projecting wings under pointed gables. The paucity of window space is notable. So too are the high oval windows with diamond panes on either side the front door. They convey so Baroque a feeling to the front that one is tempted to wonder if after all the centre does not, like the gateway, date from the early years of Charles II's reign.

A flight of eleven steps leads to a terrace on which the front of the house stands. The entrance porch with primitive sort of classical pediment, projects imperceptibly from the two-storey centre block connecting the two wings. Within the porch a splendid contemporary front door with fan-like arch, leads straight into a screens passage. The screens are surely the *chef-d'oeuvre* of Cold Ashton, certainly in so far as the interior is concerned. And they have never been seriously tampered with. They consist of two facing partitions of wainscot, both carved out of solid oak in rusticated panels within what are called fields (i.e. moulded frames). A repeated lozenge device forms the frieze. The screens may once have been painted in polychrome; but no one could regret the present faded waxed

Cold Ashton Manor, the 17th century gateway bearing the arms of the Gunning family.

Jacobean oak door leading from screens passage to the garden.

The Hall screen in the Corinthian order.

The elaborate screens of solid oak in rusticated panels.

surface of the natural wood. Two arched openings give access to the hall. From the screens passage, when the front and garden doors are open, there are marvellous views northwards up steps to a stone arch flanked by niches, and southwards to the top half of the entrance gateway and St. Catherine's Valley beyond. Immediately over the hall is the Great Chamber. This long, low room, now a bedroom, is like the dining-room panelled. All the panelling in the house must be attributed to the Gunnings' tenure. The Great Chamber too is sparsely decorated with stucco work on the ceiling. The delightful rooms in the attic all have stone fireplaces set higgledy-piggledy in and across corners, placed there by the strict symmetry of the outside chimney-stacks. From a passage in the west wing a narrow doorway with pointed arch gives on to the flat lead roof of the south porch, deliberately intended to be a view-point.

The garden side of the house is conventional compared with the entrance front. Nevertheless the three pointed gables and the setting of the small windows, as well as the chimney-stacks, preserve the strict symmetry which we have noticed elsewhere. This side somehow emphasises the compactness and the smallness of Cold Ashton Manor, which was built to be, not the seat of a landed family, but the country dwelling of prosperous city merchants.

On the death of Sir Robert Gunning in 1682 Cold Ashton went to his sister Elizabeth, wife of Sir Thomas Langton, who had likewise been Mayor of Bristol in 1658. The Langton seat was Newton Park, a large property outside Bath on the road to Bristol. In time the Langtons became Gore-Langton who ultimately gave rise to the Dukes of Buckingham and Chandos. On the last Duke's death in 1889 his estates, including that of Cold Ashton, went to his nephew the 4th Earl Temple of Stowe. In 1902 the 5th Earl sold the manor to his sitting tenant, Lucas, the last of a succession of farmers. Of these farmers the richest had been John Osborne, who rebuilt the barn in 1810 to store wheat bought when prices were rising during the Napoleonic wars. Christopher Hussey told how John Osborne filled his barn to bursting point and then piled the rooms of the house with sacks. Still he would not sell. Prices fell. His sacks lay rotting and the grain in the dining-room poured through the floor boards into the rat holes.

By the Great War the manor had just about reached the nadir of its fortunes. The west wing was smothered with dense ivy. Deterioration and disrepair were rampant. The saviour of Cold Ashton Manor was Colonel Reginald Cooper. In 1923 he bought the house and land outright from Farmer Lucas. He restored and furnished it sparingly with exquisite tables, chairs, sofas, cabinets and tapestries. Indeed Reggie Cooper was a member of what John Cornforth calls 'the ex-Foreign Office circle', a group of young men in the early decades of this century who were not especially rich but enjoyed independent means. They had a passion for buying old manor houses that had fallen into decay. They were not craftsmen, followers of William Morris or members of the Arts and Crafts movement. They merely loved old houses and had infallible taste. They did up the houses they acquired in a conservative manner and filled them with appropriate furniture, mostly oak and walnut. They were particularly fond of textiles, tapestries and needlework. Of this circle were Sir Louis Mallet (of Wardes, near Otham), Sir Walter Jenner (Lytes Carey) and his brother Colonel Jenner (Avebury Manor), E.G. Lister (Westwood Manor), Sir Orme Sargent and G.J. Kidston (Hazelbury Manor). Their enthusiasm probably derived from *Country Life* articles and their inspiration from Edward Hudson, the proprietor, and H. Avray Tipping, its architectural editor.

Colonel Reginald (Reggie) Cooper who bought and restored Cold Ashton Manor in 1923.

Having reinstated Cold Ashton to a standard of excellence which it may not have reached before and never was to reach after his ownership, Reggie Cooper stayed there only two years, and moved on to Cothay in Somerset. Fortunately Cold Ashton Manor is still privately owned and inhabited by a caring family with the means to maintain it.

Compton Cassey House

Compton Cassey House, showing the truncated wing which connected the north and south blocks. The pier and urn are visible in Kip's view (*see overleaf*).

In August 1907 a young architect, who had just completed his apprenticeship and hated the idea of working in London, took a train to Cirencester. There he hired a donkey and trap and set off vaguely wandering around the Cotswolds. All he had with him was a small tent and a sketch book. Leaving the town he allowed the donkey to select the route. After a day or two Norman Jewson and the donkey

> came to a clearing with a rippling stream running through a green meadow dotted with sheep. The far side of the meadow was bounded by a low stone wall flanked by graceful stone piers with moulded caps bearing richly carved vases. An avenue of ancient yews and vestiges of terraces and lawns remained to indicate once stately gardens: while beyond was a house of the gracious but unpretentious refinement that characterizes the architecture of the time of Charles II. One wing had evidently been pulled down at some time and the rest of the house was in a neglected state, badly in need of repair, but even so the perfect proportions of the house, with its regularly spaced stone-mullioned windows and stone-tiled roof, the mellow stone of its walls contrasting with the dark yews, combined to form an impression of such haunting beauty that it remains with me still. I was entranced with the place and wanted to spend several days making careful drawings of the house and gardens, but greatly to my disappointment the farmer who lived in the one wing that was still inhabited, informed me that the property belonged to a certain peer, who had given strict instructions that neither camping nor sketching was to be allowed. "And," said he, "his lordship is a very funny man.'"

Eventually Jewson and his donkey reached Sapperton where he called upon Ernest Gimson and the Barnsleys, married Ernest Barnsley's daughter and remained there for four decades.

Twenty years after Jewson's visit, not in a donkey trap but on a bicycle, likewise with a tent or the semblance of such a thing strapped to the carrier, I found myself, having passed through Withington village on the same narrow dusty lane, gazing enraptured upon the remains of Compton Cassey House. I too shall never forget the beauty of this relic of a great mansion built of the guinea golden stone which crops up in isolated patches of the Cotswolds – a mansion half deserted, solitary in a valley, seemingly miles from anywhere, reputedly haunted, and certainly mystic, wonderful. Another sixty years on and the place is just the same, posing the unanswered question why so palatial a house was built on its solitary site in the first place, and why and when two-thirds of it were demolished. I say 'just the same' but this, alas, is true only of the vestigial house and garden. The landscape is bestraddled with giant electricity pylons drooping thick cables. This encroachment of the 20th century upon a place previously so timeless is a tragedy. Wherever one stands one cannot, try as one may, obliterate the pylons. The timelessness of Compton Cassey has evaporated.

We know exactly how Compton Cassey looked in its heyday from Kip's bird's-eye view in Atkyn's *Gloucestershire* of 1712, for what remain of house, outbuildings and gardens are faithfully delineated. The plate is another vindication of the astonishing accuracy of Jan Kip's drawings. The house, then the seat of Sir Richard Howe (or How) 3rd Baronet, was, says Atkyns, large 'and new-built with delightful gardens, and a pleasant river running through them, with an agreeable prospect on large woods, and on a park of great extent,' and two thirds larger than it is today. It was built by Sir Richard's grandfather Sir John Howe who was created a baronet by Charles II at the Restoration. He had been left the property and other estates in Wiltshire and Somerset by a maternal uncle, Sir Richard Grubham, much of whose fortune derived from rights over an Armada wreck. Before Grubham's acquisition of it the place had for centuries belonged to the Cassey family from whom it took the name, to distinguish it from the village of Compton Abdale nearby. The house in Kip's plate was of H plan, the front door in the centre of the cross-piece facing west between two extensive arms. The north arm and three bays of the cross-piece survive; so too does a lower gabled wing at the back; and also the long stable block with its range of dormer windows and two rows of square nesting boxes for pigeons at the western end. But the great wing, forming the south stroke of the H with pedimented centrepiece and the receding extremities (out of view in the engraving) are no longer there. This south wing gave on to a paved terrace from which an ornamental bridge crossed the canalised waters of the young river Coln to a parterre. The canal, still in existence with revetted walls, still kinks to the right to pass under another bridge and lane to Compton Abdale. What is interesting is that the two artificially banked gardens on either side of the parterre survive, although the steps to them, shown by Kip, have disappeared. The two rows of little regimented trees shown by Kip are today venerable yew hedges, possibly the very same trees after nearly three centuries' growth. The circular pool at the far end of the parterre and semi-circular wall with gateway to the fields have gone. A straight fence takes their place, but the pair of handsome stone piers with urns depicted have been shifted to where the broken walls terminate. Gone however is the great layout of geometrical beds in box or yew and the gravel walks which stretched to the east of the house along the lane to Compton Abdale. Remnants of retaining walls alone survive.

Top. Compton Cassey House. Kip's birds-eye view dated 1712 of the complete house and garden layout, then the seat of Sir Richard Howe, 3rd baronet.

Bottom. The House today, and the stable wing.

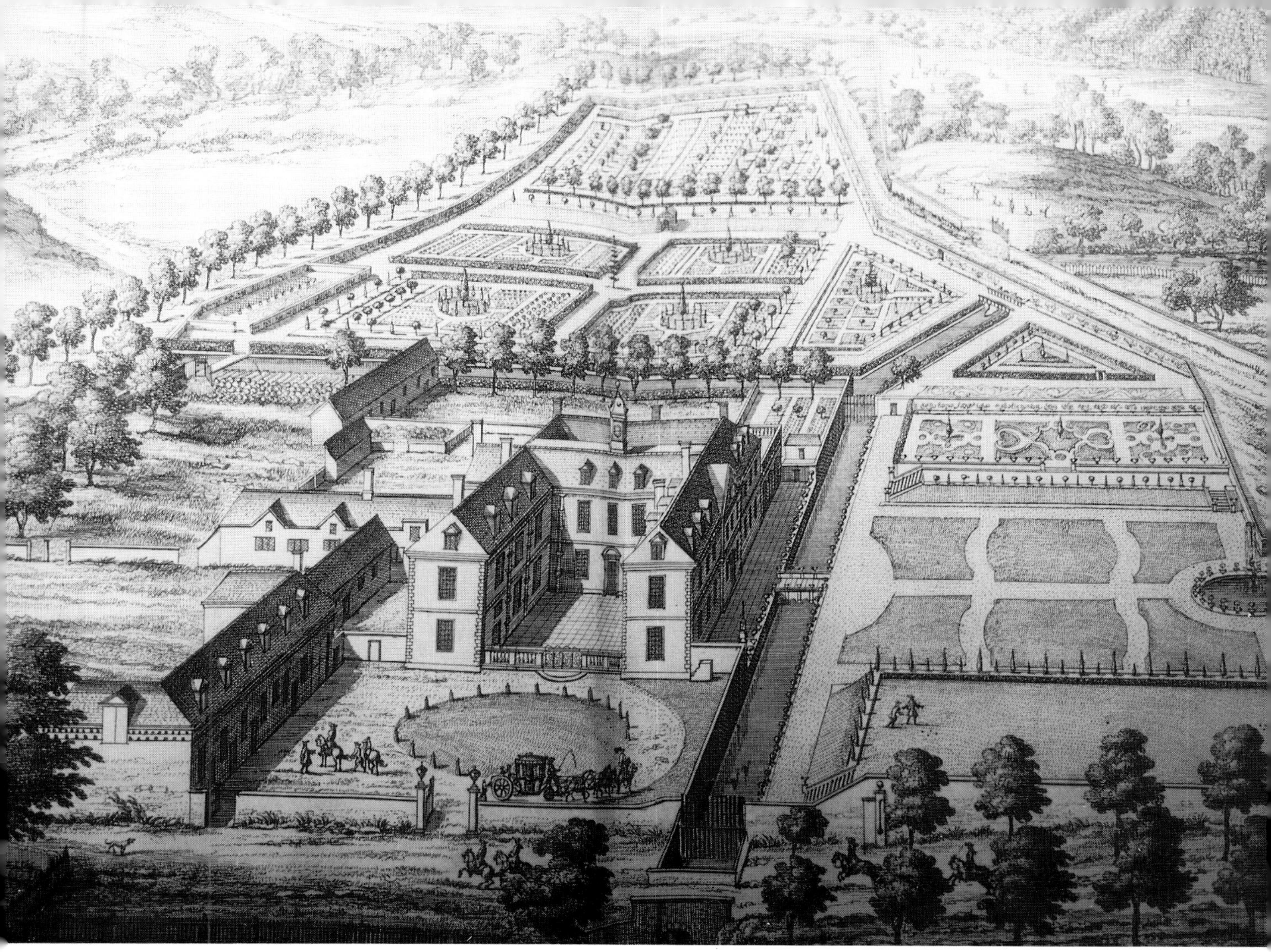

The south front today. Kip's minute yews have grown into a high avenue.

On the death of the third baronet in 1730 the Compton Cassey branch of the Howes became extinct. The estate passed with the baronetage to a younger branch in the person of John Howe of neighbouring Stowell Park, which his father had bought and retired to after a hectic and equivocal political career. From now on the fate of Compton Cassey House is obscure. Did the younger branch after their inheritance inhabit it, and, if so, for how long? What is peculiar is that Alexander Pope, the poet and intimate friend of the 1st Earl Bathurst, who had led Pope to suppose he was expecting him at Cirencester Park, was obliged instead to spend a night in August 1728 with John Howe at Compton Cassey, which was two years before Sir Richard's death. In a letter to Martha Blount the poet wrote: 'I lay next at Mr. Howe's, in Gloucestershire where Nature has done everything, and luckily, for the master has ten children. But it might be made very grand, merely by taking away part of what is there already.' This suggests that Sir Richard had moved out towards the end of his life and handed over to his heir.

Doorway and gable on the north side of the stable block.

John Howe, having been Whig M.P. for Gloucester and Wiltshire, where he also possessed extensive estates, was created by Walpole the first Lord Chedworth in 1741. In the political game of changing sides he followed, only more successfully, in the footsteps of his notorious father, Jack Howe, one time Paymaster-General who was mercilessly reviled by Macaulay for 'ratting' on the Whigs. Lord Chedworth enjoyed his nobility for one year, dying in 1742. He was succeeded by his eldest son the 2nd Lord Chedworth who owned a famous racehorse called Dormouse, sired by the Darley Arabian, and thus the ancestor of all English thoroughbreds. He died in 1762 and was succeeded by his brother the 3rd Lord. Both were bachelors. Of the last a story was told by his niece Miss Wright who lived with him how his grave doubts as to the survival of the soul in another world after this one were resolved. One morning Lord Chedworth came down to breakfast. His niece noticing that he was agitated asked him the cause. He replied, 'Molly, I had a visit last night from my old friend, B---.' 'What!' she said, 'did he come after I went to bed?' 'His spirit did,' said Lord Chedworth. 'Oh, my dear uncle, how could the spirit of a living man appear?' 'He is dead beyond all doubt,' replied Lord Chedworth. 'He stood before me in my bedroom and said, 'Chedworth, I died this night at eight o'clock. I come to tell you that there is another world beyond the grave; there is a righteous God that Judgeth all.' 'Depend upon it, uncle, it was only a dream,' persisted Miss Wright. But as she spoke a groom appeared on horseback at the door (was it at Stowell Park or could it have been at Compton Cassey?) to deliver a letter to Lord Chedworth, announcing the sudden death of his friend, B---.

The 3rd Lord was succeeded by his nephew the 4th and last Lord Chedworth, whose father had been a country parson. This peer was considered an eccentric simply because he was sensitive, intellectual and devout. Even his love of the turf did not render him normal in the opinion of his social equals. His interest in the stage, and indifference to actresses, rendered him deeply suspect. Shy and reserved, except in the company of a few literary intimates, he appeared in manner and dress peculiar. Yet no man could criticize his morals. This did not prevent misunderstandings. A stranger disapproving of his Lordship's dislike of high society struck him a blow. Lord Chedworth promptly went to law, and the verdict was in his favour. He died in 1804 leaving his large estates to his solicitor, Mr Wilson and surgeon, Thomas Penrice, 'between whom and himself had existed a long, an unbroken, and a perfectly independent friendship,' according to the *Gentleman's Magazine*. A cousin, Colonel Wright, who considered himself the heir-at-law contested the will on the grounds that the testator was insane. Insanity however was not proved, and the Colonel lost the case.

Wilson and Penrice between them gradually split up the estates they inherited and sold them. In 1811 Judge William Scott who later became Lord Stowell, purchased the Chedworth, Stowell and Compton Cassey lands. It was he whom William Cobbett on his way from Stow-on-the-Wold to Cirencester by post-chaise roundly cursed for the length of his lordship's park wall, of which he thought he would never come to the end and over the top of which he could see nothing. Lord Stowell lived in Stowell Park until his death in 1836 when his properties were inherited by the grandson of his famous younger brother, John Scott, the Lord Chancellor and 1st Earl of Eldon. It was the 3rd Earl of Eldon of whom the farmer living at Compton Cassey told Norman Jewson that his lordship was a very funny man. Lord Eldon was a model landlord but a tyrannical father. Mr. John Green of Chedworth Manor relates that his sons were allowed to shoot with their father only on receipt of a written invitation found on their dressing-tables; and that they were obliged to bribe the gardeners to rake over the drive before dawn to show that they had not been out gallivanting the night before.

Covered porch leading into the kitchen.

In 1923 the Eldons' Gloucestershire estates were disposed of, and both Stowell Park and Compton Cassey are now owned by the present Lord Vestey – in spite of John Buchan (and others) falling in love with the house and attempting to buy it.

Cornwell Manor

Square dovecote with louvre to the west of the house.

Top. Cornwell Manor, south front from the road overlooking the water garden.

Bottom. The east front from the garden.

Like Chastleton, Cornwell Manor, is just inside Oxfordshire. The two small villages are by crow flight a little more than two miles apart, separated by the Stow-on-the-Wold to Great Rollright road. Once within its orbit you immediately notice you are within a well ordered estate. Hugging a well-preserved stone wall on your right you unexpectedly come upon a wrought iron *clairvoyée* of bold Baroque squirls and curlicues, with a view across a dip of water to a mid-Georgian squire's house. Do not be deceived into thinking the *clairvoyée* is an unknown masterpiece of William III's famous iron-smith, Jean Tijou. It is nothing of the sort and dates from the late 1930s. It is none the less elegant for that. My first thought on coming from Chastleton, that highly romantic fly in amber, was the notable polarity of style and condition of these two neighbouring country houses, the one perhaps verging towards the end of its four centuries family ownership, the other rejoicing in the prosperous early years of, let us hope, a similar length of family tenure.

Until the 1930's Cornwell was a forgotten village above a narrow dell into which the converging sources of the Evenlode copiously poured their waters. More than a hundred years before that decade Joseph Skelton in *The Antiquities of Oxfordshire,* after complaining of the paucity of history attached to the village, wrote, 'at this day [it] contains but little worthy of notice, excepting the handsome mansion and estate of the Penystone family.' The Penystones indeed were the builders of the Georgian block, which they attached to an earlier house of the Annesley family. Vestiges of the latter are met with, notably a medieval tower attached to the south-west end of the house and containing a circular newel stair from cellar to attic, and some low gabled appendages at the rear. Of the Annesley occupancy the stables and manorial dovecote to the west of the house are the most conspicuous reminders. The first Penystone of any account was Thomas, a lawyer and M.P. created a baronet by James I. Although the baronetcy became extinct with the death in 1705 of his grandson, Sir Fairmedow, the delicious name of his mother's family, the Penystone surname, was revived in the female line. Of the squire who rebuilt the house no more seems to be known than of his architect. Both lie buried in oblivion. In 1875 the builder's male descendants died out in their turn and

The miniature village hall and cottages, either built or reconstituted by Sir Clough Williams-Ellis.

a certain John Francis Partridge from Norfolk inherited the estate and adopted the Penystone surname; twenty-two years later a nephew of his did likewise. Meanwhile Cornwell Manor became more and more obscured from public view by impenetrable shrubs and conifers.

Then one fine day in 1938 Mrs Anthony Gillson, a rich American lady married to an Englishman, passed by. She liked the surrounding country; she liked the isolation. She was curious to have a look at the manor-house and drove up to the front door. She rang the bell, and demanded to see the owner. She announced – so it is said – that she would like to buy the property. The owner, surprised, replied that it was not for sale. Mrs. Gillson retorted that everything in this world had its price; and bought the house, village and estate, lock, stock and barrel. She had the sense and good taste to call upon Clough William-Ellis, creator of Portmeirion in Wales, to carry out wholesale improvements and extensions to the house, to lay out the gardens and re-model the village. Being a philanthropic lady she felt she could not beautify the house for herself and neglect the cottagers at her door.

Clough Williams-Ellis was a romantic, and lover of the Baroque. He was by no means a professional architect. In fact he prided himself on being an amateur. I once asked him if Lutyens, who he said had great influence on him, had taught him. 'No one taught me,' was the instantaneous reply. Clough had, if not enemies, then critics, for this debonair eccentric, invariably wearing fancy dress, that is to say breeches and yellow stockings and an odd folded-over blue stock, shouting and laughing in a voice like a fog-horn, was absolutely undislikeable. But as an architect he had his weaknesses. In the first place many of his buildings were constructed so hastily to keep pace with his ever-changing ideas that they might be frighteningly flimsy, or even hollow at the back; and in the second place they sometimes fell down. It speaks highly for Mrs. Gillson's strong influence that Clough's work at Cornwell was remarkably solid and enduring.

It was typical of Clough that he enlisted as builders the old family of Grove from Milton-under-Wychwood, who had flourished since the 17th century and even worked for Sir Christopher Wren. The Groves disliked Modernism as much as he did, and were dyed-in-the-wool traditionalists. Consequently the model village Clough created on the hillside to the west of the house was slightly self-conscious and theatrical, indulging in curved walls ending in Rococo scrolls, bell-cotes, little cupolas, plenty of stone piers and balls and some neo-Georgian windows replacing what before was plain ugly. An unsightly Victorian school was turned into a miniature village hall and the only shop given a Georgian bow. Furthermore, on Mrs. Gillson's insistence, up-to-date interiors were fashioned, water was laid on, sanitation provided, and electricity conveyed to every dwelling. The result, with a tiny village green, is undeniably pretty and a pleasant community to live in

One of a pair of Adam-style glasses framed in Rococo stucco.

A short drive takes us off the lane (which within a mile or so will pass the entrances to two well-known Gloucestershire country houses, Adlestrop and Daylesford, of which the latter was in my youth an island of Worcestershire, although quite twenty miles distant from its main bulk) and doubling back leads us to the south front of the house which we have already glimpsed through Clough Williams-Ellis's *clairvoyée*. This front in rubble masonry is of two storeys with dormer windows in the roof; a central pediment contains an oval eye window. The only unusual feature which the architectural historian may observe is a continuous string-course which, running like a narrow belt across the facade, dips under each first-floor window to serve as sill.

The front door opens straight into the hall which Williams-Ellis made to look like an open courtyard by contriving feigned arcades along the walls, which are painted Pompeian red. A stone chimney-piece bears the Penystone arms of three Cornish choughs. To the right of the hall the drawing-room has a carved Adam-style fireplace and a pair of inset oval mirrors framed by Rococo plasterwork. Neither hall nor drawing-room has a plaster ceiling. The main staircase, lit by a Venetian window, is mid-Georgian. The oak panelling of the dining-room, brought here presumably from a room in the earlier house and partly made up, is unusual, being Jacobean painted in a feathery fashion to resemble mahogany. Over the fireplace hangs the only portrait of a Penystone, namely a youth holding a hat with a large feather of the time of James I. He could be Sir Thomas the first baronet. The Library panelling is even more striking. It is painted in geometrical patterns with urns of flowers and dates from about 1640.

North of the Georgian block and kept well away as it were from the adults' wing is a beautifully self-contained nursery wing. To the north of another courtyard Clough built a ball-room connected to the house by an arched corridor. It has high sashed windows and a bowed musicians' gallery.

It is extraordinary and somewhat poignant that after all her expenditure of thought and money Mrs. Gillson never spent one night in the house. When it was finished the war was raging. Her husband Anthony was killed fighting in the Air Force. Cornwell was put on the market. It was bought some twenty-seven years ago by the Hon. Peter Ward, a younger son of the Earl of Dudley. He maintains the house in an immaculate condition which would surely have found the utmost favour with Mrs Gillson, filling it with splendid furniture and family portraits. Furthermore he has extended and improved the gardens which were so imaginatively begun by Williams-Ellis. They are in full view of the south and east windows of the house, which looks down on them from the knoll on which it is situated.

On the east side Mr. Ward has made a formal garden of box compartments with a round pouffe at each corner. In the middle a lead statue dominates the scene from a stone plinth. Beyond the formal garden a lime walk leads eastwards to the church, which stands apart from the village, and which one can only suppose the Georgian Penystones removed bodily out of their sight. Each tree is ingeniously protected from grazing cattle by iron guards extended from the railings. The largest memorial in the nave of the church is to the last of the baronets, Sir Fairmedow, 'who died the 24th December 1705 aged 50'. Did his death cast in Cornwell a blight upon Christmas day of that year, I wonder? Or was Christmas day then no more of a festival than, say, that of the Holy Innocents or King Charles the Martyr today?

It is from the south front that Williams-Ellis's landscape is best appreciated. From the right-hand-side of the vista a stream gushes from a small arch under the road into a short canal with flagged edges, then into an oval pool under weeping willows. The pool is axial with the front door and a series of grass steps which ascend to the *clairvoyée*. From the pool the water flows into a long canal edged with silver weeping pear trees before turning into a meandering stream edged with gunnera. Once cascade empties into another. A series of pools break the line of the valley, finally ending in a large lake from which the house can be glimpsed.

Cornwell Manor. Dining room with Jacobean panels artificially feathered.

The ballroom built by Clough Williams-Ellis.

Pump house in the valley leading to the lake.

Daneway House

Daneway's origins were patrician, judging by the name of the house's earliest recorded owner and re-builder, Henry de Clifford, an ancestor of the Cliffords of Frampton away in the Berkeley Vale. He obtained a licence to crenellate a residence on the site and to have Mass said in his chapel in 1339. The site selected was in the very heart of the Cotswolds high above the right bank of the Frome brook before it veers westward into the Golden Lynch Valley towards Chalford, turns northwards through Stroud and finally flows into the Severn estuary. The site of Daneway is still densely wooded so that the present house is practically invisible, and only occasional distant shouts betray the nearby village of Sapperton.

How large the de Clifford's fortified residence was is unknown. Probably not very, since the hall, which is the nucleus of the present house, covered the same area that it does now. Daneway is said to have been a dower house let for a rent of one red rose at midsummer. Within a few years however, in 1397, it was tenanted by the family of Hancox, or Handcocks (the spelling seems optional). They were certainly yeomen. It is interesting to trace through the aggrandisement of the house how the Hancoxes raised themselves to gentlemen, though not esquires. Their descendants remained at Daneway until the 1860s.

Daneway. From the front door a flagged passage joins at a slightly higher level the old screens passage.

The pre-Clifford great hall and solar, the gable end of which is supported by 13th century buttresses, run from east to west. The hall was open to the roof and there are traces of blackened timbers where the fire smoke escaped through them. But in the 16th century the Hancoxes divided the hall horizontally. They ceiled the lower half with hefty rafters resting on and sloping away from a stalwart central crossbeam, like a ship's keel, beautifully moulded and stopped.

In the seventeenth century two irregular wings with pointed gables were added to the south at right angles to the hall. Under a vast lintel the present entrance door now leads to a flagged passage which joins at a slightly higher level the old screens passage. Up three steps to the left a trefoil-headed doorway, a left-over from the de Clifford house, was inserted to give access to what became an oratory and is now a sitting-room. The vista from the front door to another trefoil-headed door at the far end of the screens passage ends in a series of worn steps in – and out-of-doors.

Daneway. The south front with the High Building on the right.

To the right of the front door a second outside doorway, with semi-classical rusticated arch, and approached by steps, proclaims Jacobean work. It leads somewhat surprisingly into a tiny inner courtyard which gives light to the hall. Within the courtyard yet another rusticated doorway leads up six monolithic stone steps to the last addition to the house, namely the High Building, a rather overpowering tower-like structure dug into the hill at the far end of the extended south front. It has five window levels if we include the topmost single-light window under the apex of the gable.

The rusticated doorways and the High Building are indications of the Hancox rise in the social scale. In 1603 they had bought the freehold of Daneway. In 1620 John Hancox, as though to give the *coup de grâce* to his new gentility, added the High Building. It is a very extraordinary addition and were not its walls of the same weathered stone and its windows of the same mullion type, it might look incongruously out of context as it is certainly out of scale with the rest of the low and modest sections of the house. On the contrary, there is great charm in its four pointed gables like butterflies' wings and wooden gutters and spouts at each junction to eject the rainwater. The High Building, consisting of three large rooms, one on top of another, plus attic and basement floor, all reached by a turret staircase, could never have been

The first floor parlour in the High Building, called the Trout Room after the stucco fish over the fireplace.

convenient for everyday use. And everday use is just what it was not intended for. It was intended to contain the equivalent of state rooms for an old, prospering middle-class, provincial dynasty.

The High Building is also entered up steps at the east end of the hall into the low-ceilinged first floor parlour, known as the Trout Room because of a plaster trout modelled on the frieze over the vast stone fireplace. A team of little prancing shire horses and figures of Adam and Eve were added by Ernest Gimson at the beginning of this century. The next room reached by the spiral stairs is called The Porch Room on account of the interior panelled porch, meant to protect the inmates from draughts, a common enough Jacobean contrivance. The stucco ceiling is of more elaborate pattern than the one below, and consists of wreathes in deep relief within rectangular and lozenge compartments. The tulip flower, newly introduced to England, is represented in the stucco work. The Top Bedroom of the High Building has two wooden beams coated in plaster.

John Hancox's son William was a person of some consequence during the Civil War. He was present when Oliver Cromwell turned out the Rump Parliament; and the Protector made him High Sheriff of Bisley Hundred. He survived until 1672. Sir Anthony and Lady Denny, the present incumbents of Daneway, remember the stump of a tree close to the house which still bore carved upon it the following inscription: 'His Wood Wm Hancox Captain in O. Cromwell Army.' The Hancoxes were steady Parliamentarians which may explain why Sir Robert Atkyns made no mention either of Daneway or its owners in his famous history of Gloucestershire. For he was squire of Sapperton House, a mere mile from Daneway on the left bank of the Frome, which his father had bought from the Pool family at the Restoration of Charles II. Both the Pools who entertained Charles I at Sapperton and the Atkynses were staunch cavaliers, with some splendiferous tombs to their credit in Sapperton church. The lowly Hancoxes who would not be expected to have similar memorials – anyway their parish was Bisley, not Sapperton – merely immortalised themselves by scratching signatures and dates on the stonework of the house.

The top bedroom of the High Building.

If the gallant Captain was not on terms, political or social, with the Atkynses, his descendants increased in prosperity and gentility throughout the 18th century. When King George III opened that stupendous feat of engineering, the Thames and Severn canal tunnel, in 1792, his great-great grandson was one of the very few locals to attend his Majesty. This William Hancox was a personage of mark in the neighbourhood – both the Atkynses and their magnificent house had by then disappeared – and of enormous girth. He weighed over 20 stone. He was mightily embarrassed when a cheeky lad from the village addressed His Majesty without the deference due to him. King George, aware that the youth had no idea who he was, took from his pocket a golden guinea and, with his customary amiability asked him whose head was embossed on the coin. 'The King's of course,' said the youth. 'Then if I give it you, will you in future recognize me?' came the kindly interrogation.

The tunnel opening has sadly been allowed to fall into disrepair, but it may still be seen, a few hundred yards above Daneway bridge. Alas, the canal is now empty. The bed choked with mud and weeds. For over a hundred years it was in regular use. My mother, who as a small child lived at Coates, the village at the other end of the tunnel, told me how she loved watching the barges emerge into the open after two and a half miles of darkness, especially since she was strictly forbidden to do so. The bargees who had propelled the boats by lying on their backs and pushing with their feet on the roof, were at the end of this operation worn out and thirsty. They refreshed themselves copiously at the little Tunnel House Inn where they often became exceedingly drunk, greatly to my mother's entertainment.

After the Hancox family left Daneway the house passed through different ownerships until 1899 when it was bought by the 7th Earl Bathurst of Cirencester Park. He was the patron and friend of those apostles of the Arts & Crafts Movement, Ernest Gimson and Ernest and Sidney Barnsley. In fact he had in 1894 let to them for a nominal rent Pinbury Park, a beautiful old house a mile or two up the valley. When he needed to move his own family to Pinbury he lent Daneway House to the trio for use as workshops and show-premises for their furniture and crafts. He also allowed them to live in cottages in Sappterton village rent free on the understanding that they would rehabilitate them. There were a number of wheelwrights in Sapperton for the trio to employ. Thus Sapperton became, in David Verey's words, 'a fertile field for the self-conscious revivalism of the Arts and Crafts movement.'

Daneway was a humming community of craftsmen producing artefacts without the use of any machinery. Everything was made by hand according to traditional methods laid down by William Morris. In 1907 Norman Jewson, the architect, arrived at Daneway unbidden. He was promptly accepted as a member of the community and remained there for forty years. He described in his autobiography, *By Chance I did Rove*, how Peter Waals, the foreman cabinet-maker, showed him the principal rooms of the house, after which he took him round the workshops in the yard to the west of the house.

Three examples of the plasterwork in the Trout Room.

Such furniture as Gimson's I had never seen before, which was no wonder, for although it was traditional to the extent of the use of the best craftsmanship in construction and finish, it was entirely original in design and had an assured distinction which only a master mind could have evolved. In its design, grace of form was combined with extreme simplicity to emphasise the beauty of the wood. Oak, mahogany, burr-elm and ebony were used in different pieces, each of which had its special treatment to bring out the full beauty of the material, whilst instead of hiding the construction, the perfectly made dovetails were allowed to make a natural pattern where they occurred. It was a completely new style, but one that had nothing tentative about it. Indeed it had the assured mastery which only genius could have achieved.

Jewson admired too the unusual simplicity and severity of style in the large open fireplaces and the primitive and local character of the modelled plaster ceilings at Daneway.

A few pieces of Gimson and Barnsley furniture can be seen in the house, notably a settle, sofa and some chairs.

When, soon after Gimson's death in 1919 the little Sapperton community broke up, Daneway was rented by (Sir) Emery Walker, the process-engraver and typographical expert, out of whose close friendship with William Morris the Kelmscott Press had evolved. He was followed as tenant by the architect Oliver Hill. Under Hill's tuition his great-nephew Simon Verity, the well-known sculptor, began his career at Daneway where he has left his mark in some beautifully inscribed stone tablets. Today Daneway is rented by Sir Anthony and Lady Denny. Sir Anthony is a mural painter and theatrical designer. Lady Denny, the daughter of an architect, is a sister-in-law of Oliver Hill. Their son Piers, who is a painter, lives with his wife in the west wing of the house. It is nice that the long traditional link with the arts and crafts at Daneway is still unbroken and flourishing.

Dyrham Park

Detail from a portrait of William Blathwayt.

The approach to Dyrham Park down a long, winding drive from the Bath-to-Stroud road is extremely spectacular and 'picturesque'. I deliberately put the last adjective in inverted commas in order to convey what Uvedale Price's famous *Essay on the Picturesque* of 1794 implied, namely that a natural landscape should be surveyed aesthetically just like a picture by Claude or Salvator Rosa. And it happened that exactly six years later the elaborate terraces and parterre gardens which had descended the steep coombe to the great house at its foot were totally swept away by Repton in favour of the prevailing Picturesque parkscape.

Apart from the disappearance of the late 17th century garden layout graphically illustrated by Jan Kip in 1712, very little was changed at Dyrham throughout the long ownership of the Blathwayt family.

The first, and indeed the only Blathwayt of note was William, founder of the family's prosperity. Not an entirely attractive characterwith an eye to the main chance, he was favoured by fortune. Yet what he achieved – which was considerable – was as much the reward of hard work as of intrigue. 'His knowledge in modern languages, his early and steady application to business,' wrote the Gloucestershire historian Robert Atkyns, 'advanced him to several publick and profitable employments: he was secretary at war, and also secretary of state to King William III during his abode in Holland and Flanders: he was one of the commissioners for trade and plantations, and clerk of the privy council in the reigns of King Charles, King James, King William and Queen Anne.' This son of a City lawyer was highly intelligent, efficient, ruthless and mean. But he had a sincere love of literature, music – he played the violin – and architecture. He owed his start in life to a maternal uncle, Thomas Povey, a senior civil servant and friend of Pepys and Evelyn, who made some figure in society and was a man of taste.

When Blathwayt was about thirty-seven, in 1686, he married Mary, daughter of John Wynter, whose great-grandfather had purchased the Dyrham estates from the Denys family in 1571. Mary was no more than a year younger than her bridegroom and had just become heiress to Dyrham on the sudden death of her

Top. Dyrham Park. William Talman's great east front begun in 1700, the Orangery to the left and matching screen on the right (*see also Frontispiece*).

Bottom. The west front, designed by Samuel Hauderoy, 1692-93.

brother in 1685. The marriage was not exactly a love match. Regarded as a business venture it proved as successful as any ambitious man verging on middle age might desire. Within two years William's father-in-law was dead and in November 1691 fate removed both his mother-in-law and his wife. Blathwayt was left in sole undisputed possession of a respectable property and with a son and heir to carry on the dynasty which he had founded with singularly little effort and trouble.

The immediate hurdle to overcome was the transformation of the dilapidated and out-of-date Wynter seat. He set about rebuilding it on a grand scale befitting his dignity as Secretary. Only a few Tudor portions were incorporated in the new Dyrham, notably the walls of the Great Hall. Blathwayt was an extremely busy man. He was obliged to spend practically every summer of William III's reign campaigning overseas with his monarch. Consequently building operations, which could be carried out only in the summer months, had to be conducted through an agent. For this reason there is a great deal of written data from which to piece together the story of the new Dyrham. For some reason the Secretary's house was not built according to an overall plan, but in two separate stages. The strange and rather uncomfortable outcome is, as it were, two houses, of totally different scale and design joined back to back by the large hall and the dining-room.

The Dining Room at the extreme north end of the house, facing the slope of the hill, and originally known as the Slop't Parlour.

The way the odd juxtaposition came about was this. In only the third month of his widowerhood, namely February 1692, Blathwayt before leaving for Holland with the King, engaged one Samuel Hauduroy, a member of a family of decorative painters, Huguenots who probably came to England after the Revocation of the Edict of Nantes in 1685. Samuel raised a two-story building facing west, the present garden side. It has two projecting wings, one tucked under the hill to form a private passage to the medieval church, which is carried on a bastion of rough wall, buttressed by yews, the other ending in a pavilion. The west front is long and low, a serried group of fifteen window bays under a balustrade with urns and a central figure of Mercury in lead. The *cour d'honneur* formed by the wings and the *oeil-de-boeuf* panels on wings and pavilions give a distinctly French flavour to what was intended as the entrance to the new Dyrham.

The shell of Hauduroy's west front was finished within a year. Blathwayt was a relentless taskmaster who withheld payment from his French builder and English craftsmen until he had exacted the last ounce of labour from them. Hauduroy complained that in the winter of 1692-3 he was obliged to get up two hours before dawn and draw plans until two o'clock the following morning. For this slavery all he had so far received was ten guineas, without even his travelling expenses. By 1694 the rooms behind the west front were decorated. Whereupon Hauduroy disappears from the scene as suddenly and mysteriously as he arrived.

There ensued a four year pause in the building of Dyrham. Meanwhile Blathwayt's career was proceeding from influence to power. He was returned to Parliament as Member for Bath. His knowledge of the Dutch language made him so useful to King William that he was seldom granted leisure for his own domestic affairs. His salaries and emoluments increased accordingly. In 1698 he turned his attention to the stable block at Dyrham, which he tacked on to the south end of the west front. A measure of Blathwayt's advance in status and wealth was his ability to engage the services of the Comptroller of the Board of Works, William Talman. Talman is credited with a preliminary design for the stables, which were supervised by a master-carpenter, Edward Wilcox. It is difficult to believe that the engaging but extremely untutored design, in which the Tuscan order used is totally lacking an entablature and the columns have no entasis, could have met with Talman's approval.

In February 1700 the great east front was begun. Now this, the actual entrance front, facing the Cotswold escarpment and the drive down which we have come, is definitely to Talman's design. His letters and bills corroborate the attribution. The east front bears no relation to that of the west. It is higher by a storey, bolder and grander. I find it staider and rather less appealing than Hauduroy's amateur effort. It is easy to understand that it was derived from Rubens's famous book on the Palaces of Genoa. It has an urban palatial look. What softens it is the Baroque orangery, originally termed the greenhouse, tacked on to the left side and the matching screen which disappears into the slope of the hill on the right – a distinct Baroque conceit. When in July 1703 the carved eagle, the Blathwayt crest, was hauled into position on the roofline, Blathwayt's career was at an end. With King William's death he had been dismissed from the Secretaryship. The Tories under Queen Anne had no further duties for the superannuated Whig Civil Servant. A growing sense of insecurity will account for Blathwayt's prudent, and restrained decoration of the rooms within the Talman block.

Dyrham Park, the State Bed.

Nevertheless these rooms stand today as a fine example of the decoration and furnishing of a well-to-do squire at the turn of the 18th century. Much of his decoration and furniture survives intact. Of the former there are the green marbled walls of the Cedar staircase; the Mortlake tapestries in the Diogenes Room; the superb grained walnut panelling of the Balcony Room, its architectural pilasters and entablature picked out in gold; the exquisite brass door furniture of this room and the stamped Dutch leather hangings in the East Hall, which Mr. Blathwayt complained to the upholsterer were 'very ill put up and must be stretcht which can be done only in wett weather.' He never gave praise to his workmen. 'These people,' he wrote, 'want stirring up roundly and not to be overfed with money.' In the way of furniture there is the velvet-hung state bed, with a tester like the most elaborate Baroque altarpiece, and chairs and stools to match; the blue and white Delft 'flowerpotts' and tulip vases like pyramids; the kneeling blackamoors supporting shells; the dummy-board figure of 'a woman pareing of an apple', not to mention the many pictures, including Hoogstraaten's perspective which Pepys admired in the closet of Mr. Povey's London House. These and many other objects are mentioned in two inventories made at Dyrham in 1703 and 1710.

Dyrham passed in descent from one squire to another. I first visited it one summer evening of the early 'thirties, accompanied by some very cosmopolitan friends with whom I was staying nearby. Squire Robert Wynter Blathwayt was scrupulously polite but clearly bored by our praise of the treasures his ancestral house contained. In our enthusiasm I fear we overstayed our welcome. He took out a large repeater watch from his waistcoat pocket, turned to his wife who was rather deaf, and whispered loudly in her ear in execrable French, 'My dear, est-ce qu'il faut les inviter a diner?' We immediately took the hint, and bolted.

My second visit was in August 1947 when Lady Islington was tenant. She had spent enormous sums repairing – and also redecorating – the house which had fallen into very serious disrepair. She was suspicious of me, then a member of the National Trust staff, and said to my companions, 'He looks disapproving. Is he hostile?' I was a little disapproving of some of her alterations but quickly fell victim to her charm and wit.

In 1956 Justin Robert Wynter Blathwayt sold the house to the Treasury which passed it, with some of the contents and the garden to the National Trust. Although, alas, no Blathwayt lives at Dyrham today, the National Trust has arranged the house so convincingly that a stranger would never know. The state rooms are regularly opened to the public. The rest of the house is converted, with the minimum of detriment to the architecture into highly sought after flats, the stables are filled with horses, and concerts and other cultural events constantly take place in the large hall.

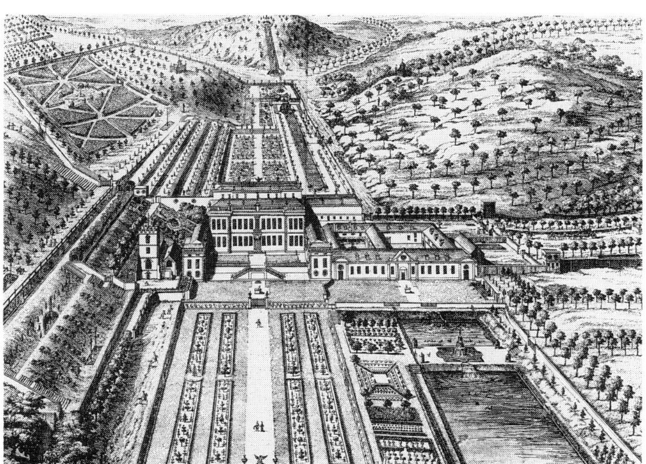

Kip's view of Dyrham Park of 1712 taken from the west showing the house, stable block and elaborate garden with steep terraces and sloping parterres.

Eastington Manor

Eastington Manor. The Leach valley from the garden.

Eastington, one and a half miles south-east of Northleach, must not be confused with the second Gloucestershire Eastington in the Berkeley Vale. Our Eastington is a hamlet in two parts, above the right bank of the Leach, here a small stream, which ultimately flows as a respectable river into the Thames at Lechlade. The manor house lies in the part of the hamlet called Upper End, which is indeed an end in itself and is tucked away down a narrow track. A barn, a group of farm buildings, a dovecote, a lesser barn and finally the tiny manor house, seen over a low wall, look so picturesque and so self-sufficient that one wonders how the inhabitants (numbered on the fingers of one hand) can ever bear to leave the place.

Eastington Manor is the nearest approach to a yeoman's house among those described in this book. Both house and garden are almost miniature in scale. Its size and tenuous history suggest that it was never meant for a residence of the landed gentry in spite of the dovecote. For this attribute was traditionally held to be exclusive to a manor-house in medieval times, in that the lord of the manor only was free to keep pigeons to glean unmolested on his villeins' meagre plots. Before the Reformation Eastington belonged to St Peter's Abbey, Gloucester, and after to the Crown. In 1586 the Dinely family of yeoman status were the Crown tenants. In 1600 Eastington was acquired by the Dutton squires of Sherborne, and for over 300 years remained part of their vast estates. Now it is the property of the Hon. Robert Wills of Farmington who himself lived in it for a time.

From the track steps descend through a pair of ironwork gates to a small formal garden with pool and fountain enclosed by clipped columns of yew on clipped square bases. Further yew-partitioned terraces lead downwards to a wood, giving glimpses of the meadowed valley of the Leach. Sheep graze round a lake which has been fashioned out of the stream.

Both garden and house are on a steep slope. The main front of the house faces south. It is a rectangular block with three pointed gables of unequal shapes and angles. The two storeys hide an attic floor in the east gable. All the windows are mullioned and have drip-stones. A single chimney-stack emerges between the central and east gable. The rubble walls and steep tiled roofs, very

Top. Eastington Manor, the house from the entrance drive.

Bottom. The round dovecote gives this small house the status of a manor.

conspicuous from the track which is on higher ground, present a marvellously unbroken surface of pearly stone patched with emerald moss. At the east end of the house, on a slightly lower level, a 16th-century addition forms a little courtyard overhung with laburnum, wistaria and lilac.

David Verey in *The Buildings of England* states that Eastington Manor (and I am assured by Nicholas Kingsley of the Gloucestershire Public Records Office that it is a manor-house) was originally a small 15th-century hall-house, open to the roof, and that a first floor with moulded ceiling beams was inserted in the 17th century. The hall was under the central gable. A first-floor room in a cross-wing at the west end may have been the solar. There are many exposed beams and the interior has been a good deal altered within recent years.

Considering the house's reputation for 'a lovely atmosphere' it is odd that until lately it was haunted by a tenant who committed suicide and by persistent footsteps of a 'fluttery' kind. Since exorcism by a Roman Catholic priest the disturbances have ceased. Nevertheless an unseen butler is said to lay out visitors' dress clothes for dinner if the owner has failed to unpack them. This sort of supernatural servant strikes me as a blessing to be encouraged rather than a curse to be eliminated

Beyond the little formal garden in front of the house is the 15th century circular dovecote, with conical roof and louvre, on which pure white pigeons preen and coo. The thick walls are honeycombed with nesting holes inside. Beyond the dovecote is a barn, partly converted into a studio, and beyond the barn an informal garden of shrubs and orchard trees bounded by a wall. An ancient stile, formed by an upright monolith of stone, allows access to another meadow with the Leach at its foot; and a pathway leads through rough grass to the larger part of Eastington hamlet.

The house from one of a series of yew gardens on different levels.

Hidcote House

Hidcote House, the forecourt and south front from the lane.

Hidcote House is the northernmost Cotswold house included in this book. It lies one mile east of the escarpment called Baker's Hill above Mickleton village and one and a half south of Meon Hill, a prominent spur, which overlooks the Vale of Evesham in one direction and Stratford-upon-Avon in the other, and which has always been the most northerly draw of the North Cotswold Hunt.

Hidcote House must not be confused with Hidcote Manor and its famous garden, laid out by Lawrence Johnston and now a National Trust property. For there are two Hidcote hamlets: Hidcote Bartrim (home of the garden), and Hidcote Boyce, which many of those making for the former pass through. Those that do cannot fail to observe on their right through pretty stone gate piers, each topped by a ball on a sort of stone cushion, the tall and impressive house dominated by one vast, spreading, curvilinear gable. It is the only big house of Hidcote Boyce hamlet, which is a tithing of the parish of Ebrington. It is not therefore a manor house, although it was clearly built for someone of consequence.

This is indicated by the initials F.K. and the date 1663 at the very top of the central gable. The K stands for Keyt (pronounced Kite) and the F for Francis. Now the Keyts were tenants of the Fortescue family at Ebrington from the 14th to the 18th century and their status was only a little lower than that of their landlords, who were and still are the lords of the manor. Ebrington church contains several memorials to the Keyt family, including a fine classical monument to Sir John Keyt with busts of himself and his wife amidst a tumble of fruits, foliage and heraldry by Thomas Burman, a sculptor of no mean merit. Burman had been apprenticed to Edward Marshall, Master Mason to the Crown, and he signed a life-size figure in Sherborne church of John Dutton (familiarly known as Crump) who built for himself Lodge Park on the Sherborne estate. Sir John Keyt was created a baronet by Charles II in 1660 for having loyally raised a troop of horse for Charles I during the rebellion. He did not enjoy his new honour or even his inheritance for long, because he only succeeded to the estates of his father, also John, that year and died in 1662. According to sundry epitaphs to the Keyts in Ebrington church they were a god-fearing and charitable lot. The first baronet's grandfather William went so far as to bequeath in 1632 the milk of 'ten milch kine' to the poor to be distributed between May 21st and November 12th in every year. According to Kelly's *Directory of Gloucestershire* this benefaction was still being administered in 1923. Sir William, 3rd Baronet, was unfortunately a lunatic (which did not prevent him from being an M.P. for Warwick). In 1741 he deliberately set fire to his house at Norton, near Mickleton, with himself inside it. The house was burnt to the ground and he perished. With the death of his second son in 1784 the Keyt baronetcy came to and end and the old family was supposedly extinct. Nevertheless in 1923 (I return to the last issue of Kelly's *Directory*) in a list of twenty-three 'commercial' residents, the name Keyte belonged to two farmers, a cow keeper, a grocer and haulier and the sub-post-mistress of Ebrington.

It might be assumed that Hidcote House, which is prominently dated 1663, precisely one year after the death of the 1st Baronet, was built by his heir. But the 2nd baronet's Christian name was William. On the other hand the 1st Baronet had ten brothers, the third of whom was Francis, a name that crops up on other Keyt monuments, together with the strange name, Anonymous, sandwiched between John and William, which suggests to me a fly-blow. This Francis seems to be our man.

There is nothing extraordinary in the younger brother of a baronet building for himself a modest house three years after his prosperous father's death, the new Sir William, 2nd baronet, continuing to rent from the Fortescues and live in Ebrington Manor. But Hidcote House when finished was more than modest, it was a substantial dwelling, which must have cost money; and how Francis came by it is something of an unsolved mystery. His wife Alice whom he married in 1657, belonged to another royalist family which suffered so grievously in the Civil War that her brother, Sir Thomas Spencer, was obliged to demolish part of his Jacobean seat, Yardington, now Yarnton, in Oxfordshire. So Alice cannot have brought her husband a large dowry.

There was a projecting wing on the east side of the forecourt of Hidcote House, presumably matching the existing one on the west. This is proved by a map of the Ebrington estate dated 1749 which distinctly shows it; on the other hand another map dated 1812 shows the house with no east wing. It must therefore have disappeared within the intervening sixty-three years. The stump, so to speak, is a windowless blank, now smothered in clematis montana.

Although absolutely traditional Cotswold the style of Francis Keyt's house is very sophisticated. The stonework throughout is beautifully dressed. The main south block carefully symmetrical. There are three windows on the first floor, the first and third exactly over two below, the second over the front door, above which a stone shield blazons the Keyt arms impaling the Spencer *fret*, 'over all on a bend three escallops.' For Mrs. Francis Keyt was

The west wing facing the forecourt. The balancing east wing was demolished between 1749 and 1812.

Shield of arms over the front door blazoning the arms of Francis Keyt and Alice Spencer, his wife.

grandly born. Her father Sir William Spencer enjoyed a first year baronetcy creation (1611) and her mother was a Lucy of Charlecote Park. When she died in 1687 she was a widow, having, according to her tombstone, been 'a lady dignified not only by her birth, but, besides her other virtues, for her love and fidelity to her husband.' The Francis Keyts having no male child left Hidcote House to a daughter Alice, married to Richard Dighton of Clifford Chambers near Stratford-on-Avon. The Dighton descendants sold Hidcote about 1750. It became a farmhouse, and it may well be that the east wing, found redundant, was then demolished.

The crowning feature of the whole house is the great gable soaring above a pitched roof of lovely grey tiles and ball finials. In convex curves and steps it rises into an ogee crest bearing a topmost globe and gilded weathervane of a kite, a play on the name. The present weathervane was actually a replacement in 1877 of the original blown down in a storm. In the sweep of the curves and scrolls and particularly in the bulls's-eye window with rusticated frame there is more than a hint of the Baroque, albeit emerging from provincial Gothic. All the windows are still of the ovolo mullion and transom type, with small square leaded panes.

The single projecting wing looking across the forecourt and up the road is likewise crowned by a curvilinear gable of smaller dimensions than that of the adjacent front.

Entry to the house is by a courtyard at the rear of this wing, through what was the back-door, which like the old front door, is made of stout Caroline oak, so hefty that it is double-hinged to allow a narrow as well as a wide opening. Old tiled buildings in the court do service as stables, garages and general offices.

The house from the lane. The massive curvilinear gable has the initial F. K. and date 1663 over the bull's-eye window.

Hidcote House, the north or garden front.

The north-east or garden front, although delightful, is not strictly symmetrical. It consists of pointed gables, each with a bull's-eye window under the apex and carrying a large ball finial. There are four groups of chimneystacks, each stack set diamond-wise. The lead guttering and square downpipes might be taken for contemporary were it not for an embossed squirrel, rabbit and owl which denote restoration at the beginning of this century by some member of the Chipping Campden school of craftsmen with their romanticised outlook upon country creatures. The great mullion and transom windows are closely set. They look across a narrow terrace to a lawn bounded by a low hedge with a small iron gate into a field of cows. Sheep graze on pastureland beyond and the grey rooftops of Hidecote Bartrim hamlet are visible on the right. To the left a field of rape was in full flower during my visit making a vivid gash of yellow across a sombre horizon. There is a pretty lower garden compartmented in beds of flowers and shrubs. I wonder if that horticultural magician, Lawrence Johnston from the other Hidcote, condescended to wave his wand over this one when his neighbour Benjamin Martin Chandler was creating it and saving the house from perdition in the 1920s.

Library and drawing-room retain their original wide stone fireplaces. The latter room has early Georgian panelling probably inserted by Chandler. Otherwise little of good King Charles II's reign survives indoors. We are told that at the turn of this century most of the rooms had their original panelling and that there were no passages. One room led straight into another. There is a chapel room on the top attic floor and a reputed hide, which, unless that part of the house was built a century earlier than 1663, cannot have been used to conceal Jesuit priests.

An owl embossed on a lead downpipe by a member of the Chipping Campden craftsmen in the 1920s.

Hilles and Holcombe House

Detmar Jellings Blow (1867-1939).
Drawing by Augustus John.

Detmar Jellings Blow (1867-1939) was the son of a shellac merchant whose ancestors included Dr John Blow, the famous 17th century composer and teacher of Purcell. His mother was a Dane from Bremen who had been taught the piano by Clara Schumann. At the age of 21 he attached himself to John Ruskin who came upon him sketching in Abbeville Cathedral. This was a golden encounter of which the student from the South Kensington Schools made the most. He travelled with the great man on a sketching holiday in Britanny in 1888 and accompanied him to Venice, reading to his mentor from Gibbons's *Decline and Fall*. Ruskin persuaded him to become an architect, and through him he met William Morris and Burne-Jones. Having worked for a time as clerk of works to Ernest Gimson he joined the committee of the Society for the Protection of Ancient Buildings and fell under the influence of Philip Webb, who was architect of Clouds, the seat of Percy Wyndham and birthplace of The Souls. Hence the dichotomy of Blow's future profession was brought about. One part of him was drawn to the simple, primitive ideals of the cottage-dwelling Gimson and the Barnsleys of the Arts and Crafts movement; the other to the sophisticated philosophies of the aristocratic and luxury-loving Wyndhams, Tennants and Elchos. The last class had the stronger pull, and in the end did him down.

Blow's charm and innocence may have been his ultimate undoing but they brought him immense professional and social success in his youth and middle age. He became almost as popular a country house architect as his friend Lutyens. In Wiltshire his most profitable commissions, Wilsford for the Glenconners, Little Ridge for the Morrisons and Heale for the Hon. Louis Greville, were undertaken in the years before the Great War. His houses were mansions not cottages, and he furnished them, not with wheelback chairs and trestle tables but Queen Anne bureaux and cabinets of *pietre dure*. Moreover in 1910 he married Winifred, a grand-daughter of Lord Tollemache, who had been brought up at Helmingham Hall, Suffolk. Notwithstanding this patrician match his wife, a woman of forceful character, wholeheartedly adopted his brand of Fabianism. In 1914 the Blows bought some land on the very edge of the Cotswold escarpment, about four miles north-west of Painswick and looking looking across the Vale of Gloucester into Wales.

Above. The original kitchen at Hilles House where family and servants ate together.

Opposite top. Hilles House from the south-east, begun in 1914 and overlooking the Berkeley Vale.

Opposite bottom. The Long Room, partitioned from the Big Hall by a classical screen.

There Detmar began building his own dream house. At first his intentions were to create a modest Arts and Crafts home along true democratic lines. He and his wife were determined to live on equal terms with the builders, labourers and tenants. There were to be no servants' quarters, no back-doors. Master, mistress and men all ate in the kitchen, and after supper Detmar played to them old country dance tunes on his fiddle. In Gervase Jackson-Stops's words the Blows 'created the perfect rural community which breathed Morris's principles of romantic socialism.' But socialism is never romantic for long. The opposing castes didn't coalesce. In eating together the stonemasons were embarrassed, the gentry self-conscious. Then came the Great War and Blow served as an ambulanceman. When peace was restored country house practice was at a discount. Detmar made the great mistake of his life. He allowed himself to be persuaded by Bend'Or Duke of Westminster to abandon his practice and work for him as a sort of bailiff and ultimately his agent. Detmar was creative and unbusiness-like; the duke was spoilt, mercurial and like many multi-millionaires suspicious and ruthless. While the incongruous relationship lasted the Blows flourished. Detmar bought up adjacent farms to Hilles, including Holcombe House, a mile or more away on the lane to Painswick, and formed a compact little estate for himself.

As for Hilles House it spread into a seat, which was filled with rare tapestries and furniture. It also became a centre of artists and Souls. Blow had abandoned all attempt at staying true to the Arts and Crafts movement like Gimson and his group of down-to-earth artisans. He became, in so far as the practising professional man can ever achieve the metamorphosis, a feudal landowner.

It is difficult to trace the precise development of the architecture of Hilles. It was haphazard. There was no overriding design. All sorts of extensions were contemplated but prevented from being carried out by adversities human and elemental. Nevertheless the spirit and flavour of Detmar Blow is still marvellously preserved at Hilles. The original drive approached the house along the escarpment from the north. A dramatic curve, now truncated, brought the visitor suddenly upon the north elevation. Whatever garden may have been has now gone. All is unmown grass up to the walls.

Suffice it to say that the Duke of Westminster and Detmar Blow had a blazing row and the latter was sacked. The unexpectedness of the break and the scandal that ensued ruined him. Detmar was in his sixties. He retired impoverished to Hilles where he died. He was carried to his grave behind the house in a farm waggon, just as he, dressed in a peasant's smock, had driven William Morris's body to its last resting place in 1896.

The house from the south-west, showing the bastioned and stalwart bay window.

Winifred Blow took over, a benevolent matriarch governing sons and grandchildren. In 1951 while she was away from Hilles fire broke out. The thatched roof and floor below it was totally destroyed. In an act of contrition Winifred led a mourning procession to Detmar's grave before turning to rebuild. This she accomplished with extraordinary success. Fortunately many of the contents had been saved, although not Detmar's most important papers. Winifred survived the piecing together of Detmar's fragmented dream house, finally expiring in her resurrected bedroom where she had re-hung Burne-Jones's exquisite Primavera tapestry made at the William Morris workshop.

Hilles House. Winifred Blow's four-poster bed and Burne-Jones's Primavera tapestry.

Apart from the roof, today stone-tiled, the exterior is just as it was when Detmar died, a long wing facing south, only one ground-floor bay window and three small bedroom windows of the bastioned west end confronting the Vale of Gloucester. Clive Aslet describes the house as turning its shoulder on the panoramic view now intercepted by the roaring M5 motorway.

Hilles is now approached from the south, through an archway where the east end of the house digs itself into the hillside. The interior is dominated by the Big Hall. This room and the so-called Long Room on the right virtually occupy the entire length of the house, save for kitchen, scanty offices and an extremely narrow afterthought of – of all things – a back staircase for non-existent servants. The stone flagged floor of the Big Hall is totally covered with a beautiful Morris carpet of faded blue ground. The flat ceiling, oak before the fire, is now of pine planks. Between two canted bay windows and a central porch which opens upon the terrace hang three immense full-length portraits of Charles II, Princess Amelia and William III. In later years this room was partitioned to make a separate dining-room at the east end for the gentry. The partition has since been removed and meals today (on formal, not family occasions) are eaten within the great oriel bay of continuous lights, which is the lowest section of a tower-like projection on the north front.

A screen with fluted classical columns separates the Big Hall from the Long Room. The far side of the screen is hung with Tudor portraits and John Riley's oil of John Blow. The whole north wall of the Long Room is blanketed with richly coloured Mortlake tapestries. There is nothing Arty and Crafty about the burr-walnut chest of drawers and Queen Anne cabinets. In this room is a small full-length Lavery of Mrs. Detmar Blow, a drawing by Vandyke and two drawings of a chubby, curly-headed Detmar by Augustus John. Among the family relics and photographs in both these large downstairs rooms a welcome oriental flavour has been introduced by the Sri Lankan widow of Detmar Blow's son Jonathan: a tasselled and colourful canopy formed from a needlework carpet is now slung from the Big Hall ceiling.

Of all the Arts and Crafts architects none had greater sympathy with or more feeling for Cotswold domestic buildings than Detmar Blow. The Sapperton and Chipping Campden groups may have identified themselves more intimately with the workmanship of the old masons and artisans. But Detmar Blow knew what the

Holcombe House, the west front from the garden.

gentry required in the restoration, and in the case of Holcombe House, the adaptation of a Cotswold dwelling. For Holcombe had never been a manor house. It was a dwelling built for a middle-class clothier of King Charles II's reign. The clothier's part in the woollen trade was to provide the wool and distribute it to carders, spinners and weavers operating in their cottages. When they had done their task he sold the finished cloth to the highest bidders in the market towns. The woollen industry was so prosperous in Charles II's reign that a Bill was introduced to Parliament in 1667 compelling bereaved people to bury their dead in wool, not linen.

Holcombe's setting in a dip surrounded by lush meadows of buttercups is idyllic. Where a narrow lane crosses a coombe on the way from Painswick to the ridge of the Cotswolds a thatched barn stands beside a pair of iron entrance gates brought by the present owner, Mrs Pollock, from America. It is built of gigantic blocks of stone and supported by buttreses. Beyond the barn a little forecourt, enclosed by stone walls runs the length of the west, or entrance front. The house conforms to a type of which the exterior has varied little since medieval times. A high and a low gable to the left; a small central gable with miniature bull's-eye window in the attic; a third gable to the right. Save the ground floor windows under the left gable which are sash, the rest are uniformally casement. All the stonework is of excellent quality whether mullions, clustered chimney shafts or gable apex stones.

Drawing of Holcombe House by Detmar Blow, showing his south extension.

The south front of Holcombe House today.

The front is near perfection. Only after one has looked carefully does one discern that the right gabled bay is slightly different from the others. Three two-light windows are united by a long continuous drip-mould. This end of the house was added by Detmar Blow after he bought the place from the Loveday family of mill owners to whom it had passed by inheritance in the early 19th century. Before he came on the scene Holcombe must have been an incomplete dwelling of little distinction. He gave it shape, form and balance. After bringing the space between the house and brook at the bottom of the coombe into the garden, laying out terraced lawns with revetted stone walls, widening the stream into a pool and planting poplars and cherries, he leased Holcombe to the widow of Lord Plymouth, who had been First Commissioner of Works in 1902-5.

By Charles II's reign the internal pattern of the English house whether gentry's or yeoman's had changed. At Holcombe the front door from the forecourt opens upon no screens or high hall, but a flagged passage ending in some cellar steps. On the right a dining hall had a low ceiling and low windows, no longer Gothic pointed but flat lintelled. On the left of entry is a parlour wainscoted in the 1720s when the sash windows were inserted. George I panelling and a pair of pilasters which flank a wide 17th century stone fireplace are painted French grey. A little closet projects from the east wall. A rich Aubusson carpet and elegant furniture, far from diminishing enhance the dignity of this little room. Beyond the dining-hall and within the Detmar Blow wing is a library, or drawing-room, where the narrow wall spaces between the windows are wedge-shaped to admit as much light as possible.

Little Sodbury Manor

Little Sodbury Manor, the west front drawn by S. J. Loxton in 1895. The oriel was then supported by a buttress.

Little Sodbury Manor is yet another example of a splendid Cotswold house built in medieval times on the very edge, or ridge of the Cotswolds. There were a variety of reasons why this was the case. One was defensive, not so much against attack, although having the rear side of your house dug into a hill made it less easy to be taken by surprise; a second was protection against the north and east blasts of winter; another was accessibility by road to urban markets, in this particular case Bristol and its sea routes to London and foreign ports; yet another was a copious water supply from the hills. A view was not of much consequence to our Plantagenet forebears. In fact a hollow was regarded as preferable to a vista. However, the view from Little Sodbury is, or rather was until very recent years, superb, across the fertile vale to the Severn estuary and the spires and towers of Bristol twelve miles westward. Today no doubt Gerald Harford, the present owner, looks upon the encroachment of Bristol's tentacles which have practically reached Chipping Sodbury, and at nights the accompanying orange lights with more apprehension than pleasure.

Little Sodbury Manor is perched on a narrow ledge halfway down the hill and just below an ancient Roman camp which Tacitus explained was erected for the Latin legionaries to withstand incursions from the hostile and barbarian Welsh. The very name Sodbury is derived from the Old English *sod* meaning south and *burg* meaning fort. Although its situation is an elevated one and the house is spread and rambling it is not very visible from below owing to the rather gloomy grey tone of the roughcast rendering. Like most Cotswold manor houses it is difficult to find, necessitating a descent from the Bath-Stroud road or ascent from the Chipping Sodbury to Old Sodbury road by a series of narrow and deep lanes. Nor is there much of an adjacent village to guide you.

A longish drive, when reached, runs due south along the escarpment. You find yourself at the front door of what is a Queen Anne block, but looks from the outside nondescript Edwardian. This is the north end of a long, low house whose best external features are found round the corner. For the house is an astonishing architectural jigsaw: a rabbit warren of little stairs and steps, different levels, inexplicable passages and rooms of canted angles, no one

being a perfect rectangle or square. You feel, on going round, like Alice in the Looking-glass House when the White Queen screamed, 'Take care of yourself. Something's going to happen!' There is that same uncertainty as to what may turn up next – a leg of mutton sitting on a chair or the White Queen grinning over the tureen before disappearing into the soup. The confusion is caused by the house having been begun in the 15th century, added to and altered in each successive century down to the twentieth, and finally given a convincing medieval flavour through a face lift by that skilful architect, Sir Harold Brakspear, within living memory.

In the first half of the 15th century the Stanshaw family built the nucleus of the house, namely porch, screens passage and Great Hall, facing west. This was of course for centuries the entrance front. Under the flattened arch of a two-storey gabled porch a flight of steps rises steeply, owing to the gradient of the hill. On the left two openings lead to the hall. This is one of the most impressive rooms in the Cotswolds, or indeed in English domestic architecture of the middle ages. The height is stupendous. The south wall consists of five horizontal cross-beams bearing close upright studs in grey oak with plaster infilling. The sharp pitch of the open roof has arched braces, moulded purlins and four ascending tiers of wind-braces. The cross-beams rest on stone wall brackets of angels holding shields.

The lowest cross-beam overhangs the screen, which consists of Gothic panels with arched tracery in the heads. Admittedly much

Above. The west front, showing the porch leading to the screens and Great Hall.

Opposite. The 15th century Great Hall.

Top. The west front of Little Sodbury Manor showing the oriel at which Henry VIII and Anne Boleyn sat in 1535.

Bottom. The north or entrance front.

of this beautiful screen has been restored by Brakspear, who also inserted the lower windows of the west wall. So too has the dais end of the hall been altered, the square east oriel being new. Above it a grotesque mask or spy-hole for the ladies to see how the menfolk were behaving themselves after banquets, is genuine. Nevertheless Brakspear's work was brilliantly and conservatively done, and a first visit to the Great Hall takes your breath away.

The Stanshaw owners of Little Sodbury were succeeded by one Richard Foster who in the reign of Henry VII married his daughter to John Walsh of Olveston. Walsh was a man of position who moved in court circles. He added the sixteenth-century two-storeyed wing to the south of the porch. This included the pretty little oriel window with traceried parapet. His son, Sir John Walsh was in attendance on the young Prince Henry and acted as his champion at his Coronation as King Henry VIII in 1509. He remained in the formidable monarch's service for many years. In 1535 Henry and Anne Boleyn on a royal progress to Bristol were Sir John's guests at Little Sodbury. The visit must have caused Sir John considerable anxiety for he was given a mere two days warning by advance courier, the King having learned that the plague had broken out in the city. However, the royal pair seem to have enjoyed themelves watching from the oriel window a tournament organized for their benefit on the bowling green.

Before this, Sir John had in 1521 appointed as tutor to his children the famous William Tyndale, future translator of the Bible into English, and then a thirty-year-old priest. Tyndale was one of the great controversial clerics of the Reformation. While an undergraduate at Oxford he formed advanced religious opinions. He was thoroughly shocked by the ignorance and prejudices of the local clergy, with whom he argued openly. Since his tutorial duties at Little Sodbury were not all absorbing he went around preaching his views in neighbouring churches. The Bishop of Gloucester's chancellor getting to hear of his behaviour summoned him. In Tyndale's own words he 'threatened me grievously and revyled and rated me as though I had been a dogge.' Still Sir John loyally supported his friend the tutor, while thinking it prudent to pass him on to another patron. At Sodbury Tyndale had translated for the benefit of his pupils Erasmus's *Enchyridion* which he prefaced with a vigorous diatribe against the vices of the clergy. Under the Walshs' roof he thought out the future translation of the New Testament, and is said to have addressed the following words, which made him famous, to an opponent in the Great Hall: 'If God spare my life, ere many years I will cause a boy that driveth the plough shall know more of the scripture than thou doest!' In 1536 he was strangled and burnt at the stake at Vilvorde in the Low Countries. A passage room on the attic floor of Little Sodbury is shown as the one he occupied.

The William Tyndale room.

Sir John Walsh's eldest son Maurice and his family met with an unusual and unfortunate calamity at Little Sodbury. Sir Robert Atkyns the county historian tells the story succinctly:

'In 1556 died Maurice Walsh Esq., together with seven of his children, occasioned by a fiery sulphureous globe rolling in at the parlour door at dinner time, which struck one dead at the table and caused the death of the rest. It made its passage through a window on the other side of the room.'

Fortunately there were survivors, for in 1608 the Walshes sold the property to Thomas Stephens who was Attorney to Henry Prince of Wales and after him to his brother Prince Charles. Henry Stephens, High Sheriff of Gloucestershire in 1635, made the arcaded oak staircase to the south of the screens passage, and put a square turret over the well. He also altered the little room over the porch, inserting the panelling. In other parts of the house he provided stone fireplaces with his initials carved in the corners.

In 1703 the north front of the house was destroyed by a fire whipped up by a devastating gale and had to be entirely remodelled. No architecture that we associate with Queen Anne's reign is now noticeable on the outside but a new entrance hall was made and large drawing-room extended to the right. In the former room stands a large central table brought from the Harford Bank in Bristol and in the latter the walls are wainscoted. Fires have plagued Little Sodbury. Another in 1820 caused considerable damage to the north-east side of the house, where the solar range was rebuilt in a conjectural medieval manner by Sir Harold Brakspear.

The Stephens family was succeeded in the early 18th century by the Hartleys, who ceasing to live in the house in the early half of the 19th century let it to farm tenants. They dispersed several original fireplaces, including a marble chimneypiece in the Great Hall, and much Tudor linenfold panelling. They removed a magnificent pair of stone garden gate piers to Lyegrove House. The place was allowed to disintegrate, some of the rooms being used for storing farm utensils and grain, until in 1911 it was bought by the 9th Duke of Beaufort. He sold it to Lord Hugh Grosvenor who commissioned Brakspear to restore it. While work was in progress Lord Hugh was killed in France in the first weeks of the Great War. The Duke of Beaufort thereupon bought it back again. Baron Francis de Tuyll the son of his Duchess by a previous husband took it over. The Baron continued the work of restoration and lived in the house until his death in 1953. It then passed to his cousin Mark Harford whose son Gerald inherited in 1969.

Baron de Tuyll laid out the gardens in descending terraces during the 1920's, the large bowling green below having always been in existence. Mark Harford was a keen gardener, and so too is Gerald, who in 1981 built a memorial arch to his father's memory. It is in the style of Inigo Jones, and the architect was Oswald Brakspear, the son of Sir Harold.

Lodge Park, Sherborne

John Dutton of Sherborne, known as 'Crump', a hunchback, who built Lodge Park.

Lodge Park seen through the *clairvoyée* from the lane.

Anyone turning south off the Oxford road east of Northleach will find themselves on a narrow dead-straight lane, apparently bound for nowhere. The prairie-like field on the left holds little attraction. Persevere, and the trees of Larkethill Wood will loom on the right. Then suddenly without warning there will be a glimpse of a breath-taking little building set behind a forecourt, guarded by a decent pair of low lodges. These were built in 1898. The little house they serve was built during the Protectorate by a friend of Oliver Cromwell. John Dutton, a hunchback, was the grandson of Thomas Dutton who had bought the Sherborne Park estate exactly a hundred years previously.

In spite of his physical disability 'Crump' Dutton, as he was called, was an engaging and picturesque figure. He was also, according to his contemporary Anthony à Wood, 'a learned and prudent man, and as one of the richest, so one of the meekest men in England.' He did not build Lodge Park to live in. For his residence was Sherborne House, on the far side of the A40 on the lush banks of Sherborne Brook. When he died in 1657 he was buried in Sherborne church where his monumental effigy shows him standing wrapped in a shroud, like the poet John Donne in St. Paul's Cathedral.

Lodge Park was erected, not as a house at all, but as a grandstand from the flat roof of which Crump, his family and friends could watch the beastly sport of stag coursing by greyhounds along the arrow straight landscape.

If ever an example were needed of the compatibility of sport with art here we have it in this flower of English Renaissance architecture. From the late 17th century until our own, Lodge Park has been attributed to Inigo Jones. Even that famous devotee of Inigo the Earl of Burlington believed him to have designed it. He commissioned Henry Flitcroft to draw a plan and elevation in pen and wash, inscribed with his own hand 'the casino at Sherbourne.' But the architectural experts now deem the Jones attribution improbable. The highly ornate facade is too old-fashioned and too cluttered for England's great Palladian architect, who actually died while the lodge was being built. At first sight it may appear classical enough. Closer inspection reveals that its derivation is more French than

Italian. The rusticated porch arcades are Jacobean. So too are the shell niches between the closely packed windows of the first floor. These are made to sit on the segmental heads of the lower, in a rather uncouth manner. No less unorthodox are the double broken pediments of these windows all running together like a continuous string course. The whole front is bristling with sculptural masks and devices and the topmost balustrade is most intricately carved. In short the builder of Lodge Park is now thought to be a sculptor-mason, Valentine Strong, member of a prolific family of builders who owned the stone quarries at Little Barrington adjacent to Sherborne Park. It is a valid assumption. The sculptor-mason may have derived his inspiration from the French pattern books of Du Cerceau and Philibert de L'Orme. He is known to have extended Sherborne House for Crump Dutton between 1651-3. His epitaph in Fairford churchyard records:

> Here's one that was an able workman long
> Who divers houses built, both fair and Strong;
> Though Strong he was, a Stronger came than he
> And robb'd him of his life and fame, we see:
> Moving an old house a new one for to rear,
> Death met him by the way, and laid him here.

Above left. Lodge Park, the entrance front.

Opposite. A painting in oils by George Lambert in the 1740s. Figures can just be seen watching the horsemen from the balcony over the porch.

Behind the ravishing little facade of Lodge Park there were originally one ground floor room for banquets and one upstairs room which gave on to the balcony. Lord Burlington's protégé William Kent is known to have provided furniture for the banqueting room in 1740 for Sir John Dutton 2nd baronet. Some of it may be seen today in Temple Newsam museum at Leeds. In the late 19th century Lodge Park became two gamekeepers' cottages until Emily, Lady Sherborne converted it into a house. This involved partitioning the two rooms and adding accommodation at the rear.

After the last war Charles Dutton, 7th Lord Sherborne and Lady Sherborne moved out of Sherborne House into Lodge Park. On Lord Sherborne's death in 1982 without children the whole estate was left in his will to the National Trust. The Trust will shortly enable the public to walk on the leads and look at the Dutton family pictures indoors. Amongst them is an enchanting landscape of the building and its surroundings painted by George Lambert in the 1740s', and which superbly conveys Lodge Park's character when the house was in its hey-day.

Nether Lypiatt Manor

There is a Nether and a Middle Lypiatt, and there is a Nether and an Upper Swell in Gloucestershire. But there does not seem to be either a Middle Swell or an Upper Lypiatt, although there is a Lypiatt Park in the upper reaches of the Bisley-cum-Lypiatt township. The word Lypiatt derives from the 12th century 'leapgate', meaning a low gate in a fence over which deer could leap but through which sheep could not stray. This does not get us very far etymologically, and as for finding the way to our goal it is no help at all. Nether Lypiatt is about the most difficult house to find in the British Isles and visitors can get repeatedly lost down the narrow steep lanes in the Stroud valleys and coombs that lead to it. Harold Nicolson, intending to arrive after tea in 1947 wrote in his diary, 'We miss the way, get lost in lanes and do not get there till 8 p.m. It is still light, and perhaps the place is actually improved by the soft twilight glow.' He may have thought so, but his hosts, as I can vouch, having accompanied him, were none too pleased.

The manor house – although strictly speaking it is nothing of the sort – stands high on an escarpment looking west over Stroud and east over Toadsmoor Wood and Bottom. When one is least expecting to find it and most despairing of ever doing so, it suddenly appears more by good luck than judgment set back from a lane. There is an attractive range of stables and coach houses, then behind a screen of stone piers with balls linked by iron grilles there rises one of the most desirable small great houses in England. 'I am entranced by the house,' Harold Nicolson went on, 'which is the only one which we have seen that I really covet.' He and his wife were coming to the end of a tour of the south-west.

Nether Lypiatt is not most people's idea of a typical Cotswold house. It is rather un-English; if anything it is rather Dutch-looking. It is a compact tall building, not unlike Ashdown House on the Berkshire Downs, which is distinctly Dutch and dates from about 1660. But whereas Ashdown is built of white clunch (or chalk), Nether Lypiatt's material is a beautiful mauve-grey stone which Osbert Sitwell compared to the colour of a guinea-fowl's plumage.

In fact Nether Lypiatt belongs to a style which was introduced quite half a century before its time. It is in the Coleshill tradition – introduced by Roger Pratt during the Commonwealth – albeit

Nether Lypiatt Manor. The entrance front from the gates.

on a smaller scale than that demolished house, and vertical not horizontal. It is an exact cube, 45ft square, with five bays on all four sides. It has four storeys in all, including a basement floor below ground on the east front, and attic, whence views can be had of the silvery Severn estuary and the Welsh mountains beyond. The sweep of the stone tiled roof over coved eaves and the symmetrical placement of chimneystacks on the roof are Pratt-like. Only at Nether Lypiatt there has never been a roof balustrade and cupola as at Coleshill and Ashdown. In place of cupola a stack, more massive than its fellows, is the central substitute. And to minimize the height of the house two flanking pavilions have been added (that on the left not, it is true, until 1931) to the main front. There is no access to them from the house and the corners of each merely touch quoin to quoin, showing daylight between.

Surprisingly neither the name of the architect nor the exact date of the house is known. Robert Atkyns's *Gloucestershire* described it in 1712 as 'a very neat new-built house'; and the rainwater heads bear the date 1717 and a crowing cock, the crest of the owner. He was Judge Charles Coxe who inherited the property from his father-in-law Thomas Chamberlain in 1699 and held it until his death in 1728. Building probably went on between 1702 and 1715. Coxe was Judge Clerk of the Patent Office and M.P. for Cirencester and again for Gloucester. He was Justice of the Brecon, Radnor and Glamorganshire circuit.

This distinguished man has been resolved into an arch-villain. He is said to have reprieved an iron-smith from the death sentence on condition that he fashioned the beautiful gates and screen in front of the house; and that because the smith did not make them strictly symmetrical he had him hanged as soon as the work was finished. There is nothing but legend to support the charge. And there is visible proof of a tender side to the Judge's character, in the obelisk which he raised to his horse in a dell to the south of the house. On a bronze plaque (stolen before 1934) he inscribed the lines:

My name is Wag that rolled the green
The oldest horse that ever was seen
My years they number forty-two
I served my master just and true.

It is alleged that Wag, equipped with panniers, would descend to Stroud, effect commissions at the shops and, laden, return by himself; and that he also rolled the lawns without human guidance. He also haunts the place in a not unpleasant way. The clatter of his hooves may be heard on Christmas Eve; and sometimes he is seen galloping soundlessly through the wood. To relieve you from being worried by these pranks it is wise to deposit a coin or two on the base of Wag's obelisk.

Judge Coxe's memorial to his horse Wag.

A wide flagged walk leads between greensward through the west forecourt to a raised terrace, up fourteen steps to a porch and front door of Judge Coxe's residence. This method of raising the principle floor was advocated by Roger Pratt in order to avoid damp in living rooms and to afford a view. In other words it was an early essay in England at the *piano nobile*. On this and the other three fronts symmetry is strictly observed. The sashed windows with thick bars enclosing three panes across and six up and down may be contemporary or a little later. Probably the windows were originally all mullioned, judging by those in the basement of the west front and those remaining on the other fronts. It will be noticed how the builder got into a fix on the south front roof where adherence to symmetry obliged him to jam the dormer windows uncomfortably close to the projecting chimneys. On this front a small forecourt has been formed between the advancing ends of the pavilions of which we saw one lengthways on the west front. A high junction wall has recently been built to enclose a private herb garden.

The front door leads straight into a hall lit by the three right hand windows. Like most of the rooms in the house the hall is lined with wide bevelled panels of chestnut wood, until lately kept waxed and glowing. The chimneypiece is an elaborate affair. The wide upper part has side trusses and an immense central swag of white limestone on a background of grey slate. To the left of the hall is the sitting-room, panelled in beech. A drawing-room occupies the whole of the East front, two rooms having been thrown together. A central partition has recently been unblocked and provided with a glazed door giving on to a wooden balcony copied from one of a pair at Ashdown. The main staircase of oak and elm rises from basement level to the attic, forming a rectangular well. There are beautiful twisted balusters, three to each tread. The dado of mahogany is a very early use of this wood. All the rooms in the house are simple, without stucco work on walls or ceilings. The fireplaces have plain surrounds in the familiar bolection moulding, and the doors high brass handles and locks typical of Queen Anne's reign.

Nether Lypiatt remained the property of Judge Coxe's descendants until the death in 1884 of Miss Anna Gordon, who left her Rodmarton property to Mr Michael Biddulph. The rest of her large estate, including Nether Lypiatt, was disposed of. The house remained forgotten, unlived in, but unaltered. After the Great War the architect Morley Horder restored it very conservatively for Mr Corbett Woodall, and put back the dormers which had been removed in 1844. In 1923 it was bought by Mr and Mrs Gordon Woodhouse. During the following thirty years it was lovingly cared for, and also became a place of pilgrimage for their host of friends. I use the word 'pilgrimage' advisedly because Violet Woodhouse was both a remarkable personality and a pre-eminent musician. Osbert Sitwell called her one of the two women of genius he had known

Nether Lypiatt Manor, the south front, showing the closeness of the dormer windows to the projecting chimneys.

Nether Lypiatt Manor, the east front from the garden.

(the other being his sister Edith). She was indisputably a great amateur performer on the harpsichord and clavichord, Bach, Mozart, Scarlatti and the early English composers being her favourites. To hear her, wrote Sitwell:

'was a great musical experience. Under her hands the harpsichord... was no small and ancient instrument, but a whole young orchestra in sound. The great and vibrant chords came rolling out with the exactness of rhythm, vivacity and deep musical comprehension that distinguished her above all executants, save such another artist as Paderewski. All this beauty however, that she dispensed with such lavishness and apparent ease, was, notwithstanding, founded on the discipline won by the hardest work.'

Her moods changed unpredictably from gaiety to melancholy, and she could instantaneously take against people. If she sensed that her audience was unsympathetic she would sometimes stop playing and slam down the lid of the harpsichord with a bang.

Before moving to Nether Lypiatt the Woodhouses inhabited other old houses. Devoted though Gordon and Violet were, their married life was not spent alone. She had an adoring court of males who looked upon her as a goddess, cherished her art and protected her from unwelcome intruders. Originally three of her 'unmarried husbands', Max Labouchere (who died of wounds in 1918), Denis Tollemache (who died in 1942), and William (Bill) Viscount Barrington (who survived her) lived with her and Gordon in perfect amity.

Violet Woodhouse can never have been a great beauty. When I first met her in 1944 she was old and tiny, but agile and rapid in her movements. She was seated in her sitting-room, at a clavichord made by her friend Tom Goff, playing a Bach prelude. She was wearing a sort of black satin bonnet, not becoming, and a black knitted dress. Luncheon consisted of one egg in a jacketed potato and nothing more. This was not unusual in war time. In any case the boiler had burst that morning and the household was in perturbation. Throughout our frugal meal Violet Woodhouse conversed with the eagerness of a child. My next visit to Nether Lypiatt was with my wife five years later after Mrs Woodhouse had died. During tea a thunderstorm arose out of a blue sky. Lightning struck the water tank at the top of the house, burst a main pipe and flooded the drawing-room, ruining the ceiling. Our hosts, then pathetically reduced to the two old men, Gordon Woodhouse and Lord Barrington, desperately searched for non-existent buckets, producing in their panic ten cups with which to stem the devastating tide. Gordon Woodhouse was gruff; Lord Barrington charming and gentle. He painted beautiful sepia drawings of the garden which was his creation. In the Hidcote style he divided the garden into compartments by great cliffs of yew hedges. His avenue of limes leading to the south front of the house survives.

There is no doubt that Violet Woodhouse was possessed of wizardry. Those who came to watch her small but nimble fingers draw magical notes from the keys of her instruments went away astounded. T. S. Eliot, Rodin, Delius, Adelina Patti, Henry Wood, Diagilew and Stravinsky were a few of the eminent artists who came to see and hear her. Poets and men of letters raved about her. W. H. Davies wrote a poem entitled, *On Hearing Mrs. Woodhouse Play the Harpsichord;* which ended:

And those small notes that run like mice
Bewitch'd by light; else on those keys –
  My tombs of song – you should engrave:
'My music, stronger than his own,
  Has made this poet my dumb slave.'

Has ever such sorcery been exercised in so idyllic an English country house?

Nether Lypiatt has, like other medium-sized Cotswold country houses, passed through several ownerships since the Woodhouse regime. Now it has come to harbour, if I may apply a nautical term as though this perfect house were a ship, in the possession of Their Royal Highnesses Prince and Princess Michael of Kent. The Princess has decorated the rooms with her inerrable taste and recreated much of the garden while laying out a spacious Rose Maze to the south of the entrance forecourt, making it a family haven where pomp and ceremonial can be safely set aside.

The west front as it is today.

Owlpen Manor

Top. Owlpen Manor. The house, church and court house (to the left).

Bottom. The east front behind a small forecourt. It is the earliest (medieval) part of the house.

Eighteenth-century county historians are seldom enthusiastic about medieval or Tudor manor houses. Atkyns in 1712 dismisses Owlpen curtly as 'an ancient seat near the church.' Rudder, coming later in 1779, is frankly disparaging. 'It is a kind of gloomy retreat,' he says before continuing to contradict his predecessor, as he loved to do, about the origin of the name. Fosbrooke, publishing just within the nineteenth century, is at any rate appreciative of the setting. He calls it 'a singularly romantic and sequestered spot, which it owes to a half dilapidated Court house overrun with ivy, a rude church, no buildings, but now and then a simple cottage of thatch, deep dells, amphitheatres of steep acclivities, clothed with fine wood, and interjacent knolls of heath.' The age of romance was clearly dawning, even to the extent of noticing the cottages of simple thatch, long ago pulled down.

Surely no one of any period could possibly deprecate Owlpen's secluded site in one of the deepest coombs of the Cotswold escarpment, one mile east of Uley, and approached by a narrow lane. The house is cosily sheltered by a dense bank of wood to the north and confronts a rising field and woodland on the south. A small church considerably altered in the late 19th and early 20th centuries but picturesque outside, and dazzling with mosaics and alabaster within, stands on a shelf practically touching the west wing of the house. Beneath the church stands either a little court-house or a large gazebo, now converted to a cottage.

The name Owlpen, as Rudder delighted in explaining, has nothing to do with owls. The word means Olla's *pen*, or enclosure. The family of Olepenne (the spelling of the name varies from century to century) was certainly settled here in the 11th century and the crest they ultimately bore was, *pace* Rudder, an owl. In 1464 one Margery Ollepen brought the place in marriage to John Daunt. The Daunts were not wool merchants, as might be supposed, but gentry with large estates in County Cork. After Thomas Daunt's death in 1749 they seldom visited Owlpen. Their descendants, mostly Johns and Thomases, owned it until 1815 when the Stoughtons inherited. The Stoughton line persisted until the present century. But becoming grand in the middle of the last century they built themselves a bigger and more pretentious house, called

Owlpen Park, on higher ground,, leaving the manor abandoned. They treated the old house with condescension, occasionally taking their smart guests there for picnics. It is gratifying that whereas the Manor still stands, the Park was demolished in 1955.

Owlpen Manor's long history is remarkably scant of incident. Only one person with a meagre claim to national interest is recorded. Queen Margaret of Anjou spent an uneasy night here before the fateful Battle of Tewkesbury in 1471. She was making a last bid to regain the throne for her sainted but silly husband Henry VI. She was unsuccessful. The Lancastrians were defeated, she was captured and Henry, who had been languishing in the Tower of London, beheaded. Thus ended the Wars of the Roses. The Great Chamber in which she may have slept is said to be haunted by her benign ghost. Her bed and chair were shown in the room until 1925. In that year Mrs. Trent-Stoughton, the last owner to have inherited since the 11th century, sold the place.

Of the three family dynasties which reigned at Owlpen we owe most to the Daunts. They built, altered and improved the house by slow stages, and they created the garden.

Until recently one approached the main or south front of Owlpen from below where a range of semi-circular steps still leads to a handsome pair of early-Georgian gate piers, carved with sunk panels and crowned with balls. A neat wooden palisade, painted white, over a retaining wall, used to bound the garden on either side. Unfortunately it and the pretty iron gates have disappeared. They doubtless dated from the time when the garden was laid out in a series of terraces and the gigantic yews were planted. Many of the latter have also gone. This means that the south front can now be viewed in its entirety by anyone ascending the garden path. Yet I cannot but regret the wonderfully enticing glimpses which visitors to Owlpen used to experience, of here a window against a silvery grey wall, there a gable on which a stone owl perches, or a pair of diamond-shaped chimney stacks above sombre old walls and sentinels of yew. On the other hand the vegetation which used to clamber freely over the lower part of the house is well out of the way.

The main front is composed of three irregular gabled sections, of which that on the right looks the latest, and is in fact the earliest, being medieval. It was remodelled and given sash windows by Thomas Daunt, the fifth of that name, between 1710 and 1720. The middle section which is harled on the outside was made into a hall with great chamber above it by Tudor Daunts about 1540. The left section was built by Thomas Daunt II, whose initials and the date 1616 appear on the embattled bay window, the mullions of which are deliciously out of plumb. Here we have a front which is architecturally a complete muddle, its stone-tiled roof lines wonderfully undulating, its walls partly of freestone, partly of rubble and partly harled, lacking any pretence of symmetry, with Tudor,

The Grist Mill, given a semi-classical cupola by Thomas Daunt V between 1710 and 1720. From a drawing by Maggie Colwell.

Top. Owlpen Manor, a drawing by F. L. Griggs from the west done in the 1920s.

Middle. A grand Queen Anne doorway from hall to drawing-room.

Bottom. Plaster detail by Simon Verity in the dining room.

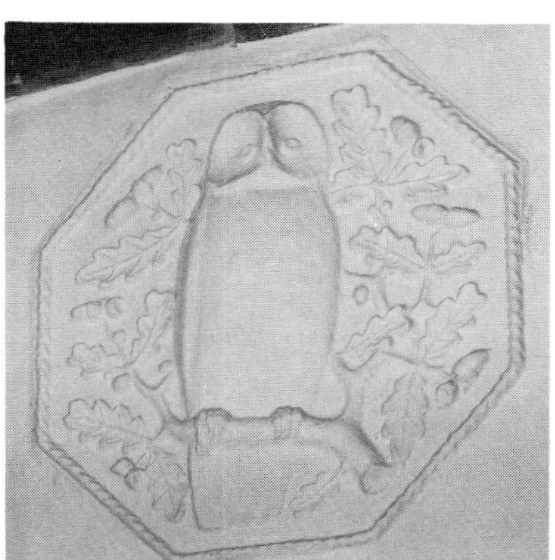

Stuart and Georgian windows all over the place, and yet a delight to witness. The reasons for its pleasing us so absolutely must be the materials of which it is built being natural, indigenous, totally unpretentious and harmonising. We admire it, not on strictly aesthetic but picturesque grounds. Owlpen is traditional, dignified and illogically satisfactory. The interior is just as appealing, and owes much to the man who virtually saved Owlpen from extinction. In 1925 Norman Jewson, a disciple of Ernest Gimson and Sidney and Ernest Barnsley, whose daughter Mary he married, learnt that it was for sale by Mrs Trent-Stoughton. He went to look at it and instantly fell head over heels in love with it. 'The house was rapidly falling into complete decay,' he wrote in his book *By Chance I did Rove*,

> 'but a caretaker lived in a kitchen wing and would shew some of the rooms to visitors ... There was also a large barn containing a cider mill and a massive oak cider press, as well as the old mill of the manor, which had been kept in tolerable repair, as the mill wheel was used to pump water up to the modern house. It was given an elegant lead cupola by Thomas Daunt V. In spite of the dilapidation of the house, which was so far advanced that one of the main roof trusses had given way, the great stone bay window had become almost detached from the wall and huge roots of ivy had grown right across some of the floors, it seemed to me that such an exceptionally beautiful and interesting old house might still be saved.'

Jewson managed to buy it for repair but could not afford to live in it. During the restoration members of the Sapperton group encouraged him in his work. The Barnsleys contributed firebacks and wall lights, Gimson helped model some plasterwork figures in the hall, while F. L. Griggs drew and made engravings of the exterior.

Jewson's work at Owlpen was careful, judicious and conservative. He had the good sense and taste (for in the 1920s Georgian alterations to medieval buildings were generally deemed anathema) to leave untouched the thick window sashes and the beautiful panels in Thomas Daunt V's Little Parlour, painted by the present owner in two shades of grey. He was obliged however to cover the floor of the room (and others) with wide boards of home grown oak and chestnut. This resulted in lowering the dado and the bases of the splendid classical doorway to the hall. In the hall he was obliged to restore the Tudor timbered ceiling and fireplace, and on the north wall the fragile painted arms of Daunt impaling Ollepen.

Under a large plaster owl fashioned by Jewson the Oak Parlour within Thomas Daunt II's Jacobean wing is entered. The bay window is latticed, and the wainscoted walls are stained in curls and squiggles, traces of the original feathering. Jewson's floor-boards, wide but thin, and laid head to tail so to speak, are beautifully mitred. In the Great Chamber, reached by a newel staircase, where Queen Margaret slept, the fireplace is Tudor, and so too are the oak door and its hinges. Here too were transported in the 1960s from another room the famous set of 17th-century painted cloths and injudiciously cut in the process. Such cloths have survived nowhere else in situ. These, once the poor man's biblical tapestry, were until lately thought to represent the story of the Prodigal Son, but are now held to be that of Joseph and his coat of many colours. The old father Jacob is shown wearing a bright red cloak over a faded blue tunic; his son a red, yellow and faded blue coat.

Owlpen Manor, a detail of the 17th century painted cloth depicting Joseph and his coat of many colours.

As an architect Norman Jewson left behind few noteworthy buildings. But there can be no doubt of his craftsmanship. 'I realise that I can't rise above the second-rate in anything I do,' he wrote diffidently to his friend Nina Griggs in 1944. 'I have never been ambitious in the ordinary sense to satisfy myself of wanting to be *somebody*. I have always been ambitious to satisfy myself (or my own standards). I suppose I got nearest to it at Owlpen than at any other time.' There is something rather poignant in what follows: 'I believe my work has the negative virtues of not offending its neighbours.'

This is pre-eminently true. What he did for Owlpen is no memorial to be ashamed of. Jewson was obliged to sell the manor to what he called 'dreadful people.' I knew them, and they seemed to me inoffensive. They did little to hurt the house and filled it with appropriate furniture. Above all they loved and took care of it.

After some unfortunate vicissitudes Owlpen was acquired by Mr and Mrs Nicholas Mander in 1974. It is once again cherished and very much a home. Stuffed with good things – including some Gimson and Barnsley furniture – overflowing with books, learned periodicals and the cultivated man's bric-à-brac on tables and floors, and scattered with children's toys, Owlpen is very much the traditional Englishman's home. Nicholas Mander's upstairs library is a philosopher's envy, its agreeable disorder undisturbed by the officious hand-operating hoover and duster.

Owlpen Manor, the west wing added to the 1540 centre in 1616.

Rodmarton Manor

Rodmarton Manor, pig foot-scraper.

Samuel Lysons, eminent topographer, was the son of the Rev. Samuel Lysons, vicar of Rodmarton in the 18th century. In *A Collection of Gloucestershire Antiquities* of 1804 he gives a plate of the south front of the manor house in a state of partial ruin. Beside the Gothic mansion is shown a circular dovecote and over the rooftop the soaring spire of his father's church. Eventually the remains of the manor-house were partly converted to cottages which survived until this century. Then they too disappeared. The present manor-house was built on a different site further south.

Rodmarton Manor was part of a large estate covering Ewen and Kemble. Since Doomsday the manor seems to have passed through several ownerships until it came by marriage to Robert Gordon of Kemble. In 1864 it was inherited by his unmarried daughter Anna. She left it to Michael Biddulph, a close friend who came from Ledbury Park in Herefordshire, and was a rich banker to boot. He had been M.P. for Hereford from 1864 to 1900, and was created Lord Biddulph in 1903. In 1894 Michael Biddulph gave the Ewen and Kemble property to his elder son and Rodmarton to his second son, Claud. There was no longer a big house on the property to reside in and when Claud married Margaret Howard in 1906 he naturally thought fit to create one.

Rodmarton Manor. A drawing of Ernest Barnsley, sole architect of the house from 1909-1926, by Sir William Rothenstein in 1913.

Claud Biddulph will have been made aware of the Gimson-Barnsley group, then earning high repute practising their Arts and Crafts revival in the Cotswolds, from his neighbour Lord Bathurst of Cirencester Park, their chief patron and employer. Whenever it was that Claud and Margaret Biddulph first made contact with the group was an auspicious day for all concerned. The Biddulphs were to become dedicated to the Arts and Crafts movement, identifying themselves unreservedly with the group's principles. From 1909 when they engaged Ernest Barnsley as their architect, until (with a pause during the Great War) his death, and the death of his brother Sidney in 1926, the relationship between clients and craftsmen was consistently harmonious and enthusiastic. It is difficult to say whether the Biddulphs or the Barnsleys took more pride in the work as it proceeded. But of the two Biddulphs it seems that Margaret played the prominent role, if we are to believe John Rothenstein in *Summer's Lease* (1965):-

Mrs. Biddulph – austerely elegant, her benevolence intermittently masked by her caustic wit – who, presiding over house and village like the abbess of some great medieval religious house, was the animating and directing force.

This splendid lady lived until 1970, to die at the age of 90.

Ernest Barnsley had met Ernest Gimson while they were articled to the ecclesiastical architect J. D. Sedding in the mid 1880s. Gimson was there at the recommendation of William Morris. The two young men, joined by Barnsley's brother, Sidney, decided in 1893 that they must leave London for the country. After a spell at Pinbury Park they moved in 1902 to Sapperton village, setting up a workshop and show room in Daneway House which Lord Bathurst generously lent them. Whereas Ernest Barnsley remained an architect, Sidney and Gimson decided to devote themselves to crafts. Unfortunately Gimson and Ernest Barnsley soon quarrelled and never spoke to one another again. Since they were all three working at close quarters at Daneway considerable embarrassment ensued. Whereas Gimson was deeply serious Ernest Barnsley was a jolly, burly fellow, very fond of good living. He took pleasure in making sloe-gin and cowslip wine and, being a gourmet, spent hours preparing feasts whenever an occasion or excuse for festivity arose. With his clients he was outgoing and forthright. His brother Sidney on the contrary was excessively spartan and reserved.

Ernest Barnsley's uncompromising determination was that nothing modern in design, material or machinery should be allowed in the construction of Rodmarton Manor, and of course Gimson and Sidney were no less determined that the same principle applied to every species of furnishing. Rodmarton Manor's value in the words of Clive Aslet 'was thought to lie as much in how it was done as how it looked at the end.' Consequently everything was done by workers on the estate, and nothing by contractors. Each man, whether carpenter, joiner, stone mason, plumber, metalworker, cabinet maker, embroiderer or porcelain painter (Alfred Powell decorated innumerable plates and dishes), saw his own work through to the end. All the stone and timber came from the estate. Since there was no hurry, the stone was sawn, and the timber, having been seasoned was cut or adzed by man power. Thus the vanishing, although not yet totally vanished, traditions of the Cotswolds were maintained. Gimson was entrusted with some of the furniture (he in fact worked less exclusively for Rodmarton than the brothers) and Sidney also with the furniture and fabrics. Numerous specialist craftsmen such as local blacksmiths, wheel-wrights, stone and tile cutters, were enlisted in the course of building. But no one deviated from the strict principles of the Arts and Crafts movement.

The Biddulphs were in a seventh heaven. They saw themselves as the master-minders of, as well as participants in a divinely inspired campaign – to ensure in perpetuity the traditional arts and

Rodmarton Manor, rain-water head of a cockerell in lead.

Top. The concave north front built in stages from left to right.

Middle. The south front.

Bottom. The staircase and chapel wing at the west end of the south front.

crafts of England. But these noble sentiments were inevitably to be aborted by economic trends, not however before Rodmarton was completed. Claud Biddulph spoke of his 'cottage in the country'. And so Rodmarton began as one, which we can detect in the first twin-gabled bays of the entrance front, so long as we obliterate the rest of the astonishing hemicycle that followed suit. Ernest Barnsley started at the east end, behind which is the kitchen court, a modest and quite cottagey affair. Gradually he beguiled Claud Biddulph into extensions, one after the other, the front finally terminating in a chapel at the west end. Although the house is really one room deep with a long connecting passage or gallery on two floors the north front became a conglomeration of attached cottages forming a crescent. The extraordinary thing is how satisfactory a crescent the north front makes. Its serried segment of irregularly grouped pointed gables led *The Builder* of 1907 to compare it rather unkindly to an upturned and magnified saw. The oval sweep of lawn in the forefront acts as a sort of village green, and a segmental belt of lime trees on the facing side beautifully compliments the elliptical facade. All the separate units of the front are so vernacular and so immaculately derivative that a stranger could easily be deceived into assuming them to be genuine Tudor. Only the canted junctions of the parts reveal 20th-century composition.

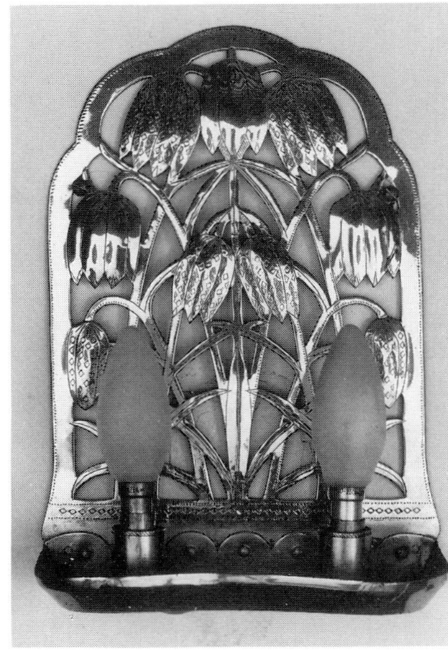

Light sconce in brass designed by Ernest Gimson.

Next to the kitchen unit came the Biddulph's private quarters marked by three loftier gables each containing a roundel window; then a central block higher still, of five pointed gables including a projecting porch. This block by itself would make a good-sized manor house; and to the west of it the chapel range. Excellent gutters, hopper heads and downpipes, adorned with owls, cockerels, rabbits and donkeys are the work of Norman Jewson who in 1911 helped superintend, and F. W. Troup, a long-standing member of the S.P.A.B. committee, whom I when a young member vividly recall as a venerable greybeard with a dreamy, faraway look.

A panel of Hilda Benjamin's applique hangings, *The Archery Team*, depicting the Biddulphs, Vicar and village notables.

The garden front is not convex as one might suppose from the concave entrance front, and the symmetrical centre block projects prominently from its east and west extremities, the former being partially concealed by trees and shrubs. It is U-shaped. From the upstairs rooms distant views are had across the flat plain to the blue tinted Wiltshire Downs. The whole ground floor – with pair of bay windows – between the U strokes is occupied by what was the hall and is now the library. It is a very long apartment, the walls three-quarter panelled and the low ceiling supported by a series of stout cross beams. Here a sofa and chairs with cabriole legs by Alfred Powell are traditionally mid-Georgian. The dining-room fills the east projecting U stroke. For a recess Sidney Barnsley designed a dresser in 1924, and the long solid table in oak. To reach the dining-room food had to pass through the Biddulph's private quarters from the kitchen block, which was not a wholly satisfactory arrangement. The dining-room was balanced by the

The Chapel with curved roof braces and pews of utmost simplicity.

drawing-room in the west projecting stroke. This apartment was used as a workroom by the Rodmarton craftsmen in early days. Here Hilda Benjamin (later Sexton) designed the textiles and her Rodmarton Women's Guild worked curtains and appliqué hangings (among the series the Archery Team depicting the Biddulphs, vicar and village notables is enchanting). The furthermost western extremity of the house, sharply returned from the gabled U-block, displays the least orthodox architecture of the house. Irregular wings make a picturesque complex of loggias (the one intended as an open air bedroom for the hardy Biddulphs having been filled in) to catch the setting sun, a vast chimney breast, a window canted across an angle and a very high window lighting the main staircase. The chapel within this complex is in my opinion the finest apartment of the house. The starkness of the architecture is relieved only by the curved roof braces with white plaster fillings and the wondrously simple pews, made like everything else on the estate. The altar, a block of white stone carved in low relief by a local mason and dated 1928, stands as a sort of final gesture of devotion to the great house, by then completed.

Above left. Rodmarton Manor. Dresser made in 1924 on the estate to Sidney Barnsley's design.
Above. Rocking-chair, designed by Ernest Gimson.
Below. Oak chest, designed and made by Sidney Barnsley, the chamfers derived from wheelwright's work.

Rodmarton Manor is without question the best memorial to the Arts and Crafts movement. In architecture and contents throughout it is a unit. I must confess to an ingrained prejudice against the arty-craftiness of much furniture of the Cotswold school. Whenever I have come elsewhere upon isolated objects of furniture with their self-conscious roughness and honesty, notably in rude chamfering of chests, exaggerated dovetailing of benches and wishbone stretchers of tables, I have been irritated. All very well for farm carts, corn-bins and hay-rakes. The truth is these cottagey artefacts (and the sad sequel was that only the rich could afford to buy what the Arts and Crafts folk produced with such time-consuming skill) do not mix well with Queen Anne, not to mention Robert Adam and Louis Quinze commodes and *fauteuils*. On the other hand seen altogether at Rodmarton, in the natural woods, unstained but waxed and polished, against white-washed walls, sun-bleached panelling and dowel-pegged timbers, they come into their splendid, honest-to-God own. The exceptional joiner, well represented at Rodmarton, is the Dutchman Peter Van der Waals, who in 1900 answered an advertisement by Gimson and came to Cirencester, never to leave the neighbourhood. His exquisitely finished marquetry pieces would not look out of place amongst the most sophisticated furniture of the 18th Century *ébénistes*.

Arcade of the kitchen-court, with dovecote.

Ernest Barnsley must also be accredited with the basic layout of the garden. His aim was to extend the house into the landscape, by planning the garden into separate compartments or rooms, anticipating what Lawrence Johnston so signally achieved at Hidcote. Thus the compartments confined largely by yew hedges in place of rubble walls fan outwards from terraces in a formal fashion. The planting which owes its fame to the present chateleine, Mrs. Anthony Biddulph, is recorded in current horticultural books by the dozen.

C. R. Ashbee, no mean judge since he was founder of the Chipping Campden Guild of Handicraft, summed up the outstanding merits of Rodmarton Manor after a visit in 1914 twelve years before it was finished:

'I've seen no modern work equal to it, nothing I know of Lutyens or Baker comes up to it. And when I ask why I find the answer in the system, the method rather than the man. It is a house built of confidence and Barnsley has been allowed a free hand to put all his personal knowledge and technique into the work.'

One of the entrances, with its tapestry hedges and pair of lodges.

Sezincote

Top. Sezincote, the entrance front surmounted by the central onion-shaped dome.

Bottom. The long concave greenhouse ending in a pavilion with high Moorish windows.

Sezincote derives its name from the old English *cisen,* meaning gravelly, and will have nothing to do with Sir Robert Atkyns's derivation in his great 18th-century tome on Gloucestershire: *seisin* from *chesne,* meaning an oak, and *coed* a wood. The latter deduction is more poetical even if conjectural. Sir Robert was not privileged to see the Sezincote of today because it had not yet been created. Nor did he describe its predecessor. Instead he dwelt upon the dreadful iniquity of an Elizabethan owner of the manor, one Ludovic Grevill. 'God's revenge upon it,' he declared somewhat unctuously, 'ought to be published to posterity.' One of Grevill's retired servants, named Webb, became rich. Grevill invited him to stay. Having forged a will purporting to leave all Webb's money to his host Grevill suborned an employee to murder him. A second employee, learning of this dastardly act, threatened to report his master to the authorities. Grevill merely bribed another servant to murder this man too. Grevill was ultimately arraigned and executed. So it seems that God's revenge was fulfilled.

Ludovic Grevill can never in his wildest dreams have imagined the Sezincote which three hundred years later was to arise like an oriental exhalation out of a Cotswold escarpment. In 1795 the Sezincote estate was purchased by Colonel John Cockerell, a Colonel in the East India Company's service and one time Quartermaster-General to Lord Cornwallis. In 1798 he died leaving his new estate equally between his younger brothers, Charles who was to become a baronet in 1809 and had also lived in India, and Samuel Pepys, the architect, who had designed neighbouring Daylesford House for Warren Hastings in the 1790's.

The Cockerell brothers were, though in a humbler capacity than Hastings's, rich nabobs. And Indian of a sort was the architectural style they chose for the baronet's new residence. It was a very novel style, but one occasionally flirted with at the turn of the 19th century. Actually Daylesford does not come within this category in spite of the high pointed finial of its mildly Muslamic dome. Hope End in Herefordshire is the only other essay at a country house in the full-blown oriental style that comes to my mind. It was built for Edward Barrett, a rich sugar planter from Jamaica between 1810 and 1815 by J. C. Loudon, and was the birthplace of Elizabeth Barrett Browning. In a letter to her husband she described it as a 'Turkish house crowded with minarets and domes, and cro' ned with metal spires and crescents.' In 1786 Sir Joshua Reynolds suggested that 'the barbaric splendour of Asiatic buildings might possibly, in the same way that Italian landscape paintings and Gothic architecture had influenced Vanbrugh's designs, furnish an architect, not with models to copy, but with hints of composition and general effect.' But 'the sound rules of the Grecian architecture [were] not to be lightly sacrificed.' The Cockerell brothers took him at his word. Out of a beautiful golden stone they produced an anglicized version of the Hindu on the exterior of Sezincote, while keeping, the interior strictly Grecian, or at least classical. In this picturesque composition Samuel Pepys was helped, and certainly inspired by Thomas and his nephew William Daniell's drawings and sketches of Indian buildings, some of which are displayed in the house today.

If the house was conceived in 1805 then the gardens were begun before building started. And they too were largely designed by the Daniells, in concert with Humphrey Repton, to whom the park and lake below the house were entrusted in 1804. The Daniell's Indian layout quickly confronts the visitor, for the drive crosses an Indian bridge spanning a dell which is watered by a copious spring from the steep hill. The bridge's octagonal columns were copied from the Elephanta Caves; sacred bulls of Coade Stone crouch on the balustrade. At the head of the ravine is the Temple Pool, so named after the Hindu shrine which holds a statue of Souriya, the Sun Goddess, recently restored. Below the bridge is the Snake Pool where a three-headed snake coils round a tree trunk and spouts water from its mouths. Below that again is the Island Pool. An aquatint by John Martin depicts this pool and ravine with the bridge in the middle distance exactly as they are today.

Repton was so impressed with the Daniell's landscaping of the ravine that he induced the Prince Regent, by whom he was being consulted on plans for the Brighton Pavilion, to pay a visit to Sezincote in 1807. Unfortunately, owing to the engineer having omitted to connect the pipes, the snake fountain failed to function on the occasion. Notwithstanding this disappointment the Prince largely modelled the Pavilion on Sezincote, which can claim to be its progenitor.

Continuing down the drive we shortly reach the house endways on. From this angle it is not particularly impressive. The north end of the main block has attachments which tuck themselves under abruptly rising round to the west. The wing terminates in an octagonal pavilion which once served as Sir Charles Cockerell's tent bedroom. It disintegrated several years ago and the spears which held up the roof have been incorporated into an immense state bed, now in the main block.

'One lodge is Tudor, one in Indian style,' wrote John Betjeman. This seems to be in both.

Detail of an aquatint by John Martin of the Indian bridge.

The Hindu shrine holding a statue of Souriya, the Sun Goddess.

Farm buildings, combining Moghul and Cotswold features.

The dairy, half oriental and half western.

Aquatint by John Martin of the front door, the glass panels reflecting the lake and landscape.

The house itself is low, almost bungalowish, with lightly raised roofs. Until one looks closely into the detail one's attention is rivetted upon the central onion-shaped dome, sheathed in verdigris-coloured lead and pointing to the skies with a long spiky finial. The dome rides upon a square platform poised upon a rather squat tower. At the far corners of the tower are slim *chattris*. The skyline is a perplexing medley of these minaret-like features, some of which are made of copper. The pronounced *chujjah*, or cornice, enhances the Indian effect. It is extraordinary that these Mongul ornaments, pinnacles and pots were all carved by native Cotswold masons.

Passing the east front, with its recessed fretwork centre and raised eyebrow segments over the windows, we get to the south front. This is the far end of the rectangle. It is bowed and verandahed, with a lace-like balustrade. Both this balustrade and the railings before the east front are made of cast iron, painted turquoise. From the south front stretches westward a long concave greenhouse, or corridor, ending in another octagonal pavilion with high Moorish windows. Behind it rises a detached object whose practical use was a chimney to the greenhouse heating system and ostensible purpose a memorial to the 1st Duke of Wellington's victories.

Further south, behind a knoll, are farm buildings, a dairy and gardener's bothy, combining Moghul and Cotswold features.

The front door, of which John Martin made an aquatint with a reflection in the glass panels of the lake and landscape, leads to a low hall where two of Daniell's large oil paintings of Sezincote hang. As I have said, there is not a trace of the orient in the decoration of the interior. Straight ahead one is confronted by an ingenious and very graceful staircase. It rises in two curving flights to return in a single arched span, sustained by pierced metal girders. It is lit from above by two lunette windows under the dome, which is supported by fan-like triangular spaces, known as pendentives.

All the rooms on the first floor are higher than those on the lower. This is the long-tried Palladian custom of providing state rooms on a *piano nobile*. In so novel and eccentric a house, the adherence to such an old-fashioned practice is curiously anachronistic. The staircase, its walls now hung with Aubusson tapestry panels, leads straight into the great saloon. It is a splendid airy apartment with a coved ceiling in trellis pattern. Two out of the original four mirrors with gilded crests on a background of red plush remain in place; and the great bow windows are draped with yellow curtains gathered by a central eagle in flight and looped from lion masks, all gilded.

Sir Charles lived at Sezincote until 1837 when he was succeeded by his son Charles, 2nd Baronet. On the expectation of inheriting the neighbouring Northwick Park house and estate through his mother Harriet Rushout, who was a daughter of the 1st Lord Northwick, he changed his name to Rushout. But when the last

Lord Northwick died in 1887 the estate, owing to some slip of a solicitor's pen, went to Lord Edward Spencer-Churchill by mistake. The expense of a prolonged lawsuit resulted in Sir Charles Rushout having to sell Sezincote – a terrible example of the recurrent mischiefs brought about by the pedantry of the legal phraseology. In 1888 it was acquired by James Dugdale.

In the early 1930s Sezincote belonged to his son Colonel Arthur Dugdale and his enchanting, beautiful and idiosyncratic wife, Ethel. In that decade Sezincote was very different from the spruce place it is today. It resembled an Irish country house, a trifle down at heel, a little chaotic, very dog-ridden, but cosy, the sort of house one reads about in a Mary Keane novel. The Dugdales' only son John, subsequently Labour M.P., was our contemporary and friend. John Betjeman was a frequent visitor and no description conjures up the flavour of the old Sezincote more nostalgically than that in his long poem, *Summoned by Bells*:

> Oxford May mornings! When the Prunus bloomed
> We'd drive to Sunday lunch at Sezincote:
> First steps in learning how to be a guest,
> First wood-smoke-scented luxury of life
> In the large ambience of a country house…
> Down the drive,
> Under the early yellow leaves of oaks;
> One lodge is Tudor, one in Indian style.
> The bridge, the waterfall, the Temple Pool –
> And there they burst on us, the onion domes,
> *Chujjahs* and *chattris* made of amber stone:
> 'Home of the oaks,' exotic Sezincote!
> Stately and strange it stood, the Nabob's house,

Sezincote. The double flight staircase returning in a single arched span, sustained by pierced metal girders.

The drawing room with bowed windows is, in contrast with the exterior, purely classical.

Indian without and coolest Greek within.
Looking from Gloucestershire to Oxfordshire;
And, by supremest landscape-gardener's art,
The lake below the eastward slope of grass
Was made to seem a mighty river-reach
Curving along to Chipping Norton's hills.
   Crackle of gravel! in the entrance-hall
Boot-jacks and mattocks, hunting macintosh,
And whips and sticks and barometric clock
Were Colonel Dugdale's; but a sheaf of bast
And gardening-basket told us of his wife...
   Dear Mrs. Dugdale, mother of us all,
In trailing and Edwardian-looking dress,
A Sargent portrait in your elegance,
Sweet confidante in every tale of woe!
She and her son and we were on the Left,
But Colonel Dugdale was Conservative.
From one end of the butler-tended board
The Colonel's eyes looked out towards the hills,
While at the other end our hostess heard
Political and undergraduate chat.

Sezincote. The house from the garden with *chattris* at the corners. It is bowed and verandahed, with a lace-like metal balustrade.

'Oh Ethel,' loudly Colonel Dugdale's voice
Boomed sudden down the table, 'that manure –
I've had it shifted to the strawberry-beds.'
'Yes, Arthur... Major Atlee, as you said,
Seventeen million of the poor Chinese
Eat less than half a calory a week?'...
The onion-dome which listened all the time
To water filling after-tennis baths,
To water splashing over limestone rock
Under the primulas and thin bamboo,
The cottages and lanes and woods and paths
Are all so full of voices from the past
I do not dare return.

Other voices, no less clear and confident, ring round Sezincote today. In 1944 John Dugdale sold the estate to Sir Cyril and Lady Kleinwort who restored the house, made improvements to suit post-war living conditions, brought back as many of the Daniell pictures as they could find, retrieved the gardens and generally re-edified the whole place in the most sensitive manner. They passed it on to their daughter, Mrs. David Peake, who now lives there with her husband. Happy Sezincote! It is impossible to suppose that this Nabob extravaganza has ever been a melancholy home since Ludovic Grevill was carried off to the gallows from its predecessor.

Sheldon Manor

Sheldon Manor. The 13th century porch.

Although perilously close to Chippenham town and actually within the civil parish of 'Chippenham Without', Sheldon Manor is hidden in flat, wooded North Wiltshire country with glimpses of blue Downs in the distance. A lime avenue leads you to the house, so obscured that you may think there is little to see, and turn away. That would be a very great mistake. Instead you park your car, provided it is a Thursday or a Sunday, in a field, and at the drive gate buy a ticket which admits you to an enchanted garden and an enchanting manor-house where you are free to wander at will and where incidentally you can get the best luncheon imaginable in the stables amongst gutted loose-boxes, hay-racks, mangers and Edwardian portraits of the owner, Major Martin Gibbs's infinite number of uncles, painted when boys in knickerbockers.

The front of the house is approached by a forecourt of two terraced levels enclosed by stone walls. Stone Queen Anne gate-piers were at the beginning of this century provided with a magnificent pair of wrought iron gates with spear-tipped rails. On the top terrace three 60ft-high yew trees, claiming to be 700 years old, tower above the three gables of the front. On the right is a small detached chapel with Perpendicular tracery windows dating from the 15th century. In it four of Major and Mrs. Gibb's children have been married. On the left, connected to the house by a low corridor of 17th-century date and ancient cow-standings, is a long projecting wing which forms a secondary court. The north end of this wing was converted in 1968 with notable taste and tact to cottages by Mr. Oswald Brakspear; the adjoining south end was built in 1723 as a barn, later turned into loose boxes where now you eat.

The three gabled blocks which form the house nicely illustrate Sheldon's remote history. First and foremost the central projecting porch is the oldest section. It is the finest domestic porch in Wiltshire: a magnificent affair with double pointed entrance arch and a Gothic window to light the parvise, or priest's room above. The heavily ribbed stone vault of the entrance necessitated the support of two pairs of corner buttresses, given pointed copings like monks' cowls. The venerable porch was built for Sir Godfrey Gascelyn who acquired Sheldon through marriage in the 13th century. The Gascelyns were a medieval family of Norman extraction and Sir Godfrey was high in the service of King Henry III. With Sheldon they assumed the lordship, or liberty of the Hundred of Chippenham which gave the family an influence over the township. Through the Gascelyns Chippenham obtained the right to two fairs each year which brought it much prosperity.

The porch is all that remains of the Gascelyn ancestral home which must have extended westwards. Strictly speaking, it is out of scale with the flanking wings, like too prominent a nose between bulging cheeks. It is haunted by a party of royalist horsemen who, after the Battle of Lansdown in 1643, watered their horses late at night at a trough kept inside the door. The Gascelyns, unlike succeeding owners, made Sheldon their home and were not absentee landlords. By the early 15th century they were extinct. A daughter Christina Gascelyn took Sheldon in dowry to one Edward Hales, an esquire in the service of the Black Prince. Then in her widowhood Christina sold Sheldon to Walter Lord Hungerford of Farleigh and Heytesbury, Lord High Treasurer of England. That was in 1431.

The Hungerfords were a greater family than the Gascelyns, Thomas de Hungerford becoming in Edward III's reign the first Speaker of the House of Commons. Walter Lord Hungerford his son, the purchaser of Sheldon was a Knight of the Garter, fought at Agincourt where he took Charles Duke of Orleans prisoner and became an executor of Henry V. He never intended to make Sheldon a home and farmed it out like other appendages of his large estates. But before his death and burial in Salisbury Cathedral in 1449 he added the right-hand block to the porch. On the ground floor of this wing is a dining-room with tie-beam ceiling, wide fireplace and linenfold panelling. Behind the original first-floor Gothic window is a great chamber, open to the roof, and now the library. The Hungerfords were too great to avoid impliation in the Wars of the Roses, which cost some of them their heads and some their estates fighting for the Lancastrians. Sheldon was frequently attainted, but not for long. There were other perils for the family ahead. In 1541 Lord Hungerford of Heytesbury was beheaded for committing unnatural vice. Finally Sir Edward Hungerford, 'attaching himself to the dissolute court', in the words of S. J. Elyard [*Some Old Wiltshire Homes,* 1894] of Charles II, 'commenced a career of extravagance that soon began to tell on his princely revenues.' He is said to have spent 500 guineas on a wig for a court ball. Sheldon was the first of thirty manors to be disposed of in 1684. In spite of his regrettable mode of life this Hungerford spendthrift reached the age of 115, outliving an uninteresting son and grandson, and bringing the male line of his family to an end. But before this happened the neglected and decaying house had a respite in a tenant called William Foster.

Foster had permission to restore and rebuild. He was responsible for the left block and much besides, in the middle of the 17th century. We can judge the period by the cross windows. Foster's

Top. Sheldon Manor. A bird-'s eye view of the house, garden and farm-buildings.

Bottom. The entrance front from the gates.

alterations inside were considerable. He may have removed Sir Godfrey Gascelyn's high hall, if it had not already tumbled down, replacing it by a long low hall (actually made into two small rooms in 1710) and leaving the east side of the screens passage with two entrances to what had been back regions. He also made the beautiful staircase with flat, perforated balusters, rusticated string, finials and dog-gate. When William Foster died in 1672 an inventory of his chattels was taken. The best chamber had hangings 'of blue linsey woolsey streaked with white, a bedstead, mattress and quilt; a cupboard, a little cupboard and a yew cupboard; a little round table, a little yew table; divers stools and divers little pictures.' Rooms of the lesser gentry in Stuart times were uniformly sparse. At some time Mr. Foster's wing began to subside and had to be supported at the outside corner by another buttress. The west bedroom actually settled several feet as we can judge by the distinct tilt of the ceiling towards the top of the Queen Anne panelling.

In 1711 William Norris was owner. It was he who erected the gate-piers to the forecourt; and also the barn. It is probable that he crowned the centre gable with the three-faced stone sundial, set askew to the front so as to conform to the points of the compass. Now that the painted digits have disappeared we cannot tell what o'clock the gnomons are pointing at without climbing a ladder or using binoculars.

The last Norris owner of Sheldon died in 1828. For years he had been a total recluse. He suffered from erysipelas and would allow no one to see him. His servants prepared and left food for him before they went to bed; and after dark the master ventured to walk about the grounds. When he died his neighbours flocked to examine the corpse. His great-nephew and great-niece sold the estate in 1854. Other owners came and went. Sheldon was let to more farm tenants. There is a photograph of it as a farm house, complete with horse and waggon, taken in 1899. In 1911 it was bought by Captain F. Bailey, the first owner to re-convert the house into a gentleman's residence. Finally in 1917 it was bought by Henry Martin Gibbs of Barrow Court, Somerset, and grandfather of the present owner, Major Martin Gibbs.

House and garden are everything that an English manor should be. Since Major Gibbs's grandfather collected furniture all his life Sheldon Manor is full of interesting and beautiful contents. But they are not treated as museum pieces. Far from it. They jostle with the homeliest objects. From the moment you enter the porch where swallows are nesting on top of the lantern you will find rows of Nailsea glass walking-sticks cheek by jowl with birthday greeting cards painstakingly fabricated by grand-children. Narwhal tusks and African drums abound. Comfortable sofas are draped with saddle-bags bought in Khuzistan. Porcelain tea services and Georgian silver nestle against Toby jugs of Winston Churchill and Puss-in-Boots. Book shelves groan with the weight of Vicary

Gibbs's *Complete Peerage* and Henty's novels. In fact the pervasive flavour of Sheldon is a cosy Edwardian clutter. The Italian old masters and English water-colours and the family silhouette portraits are put into the shade by the dominant picture by John Calcott Horsley, R.A. (known to contemporary artists as Clothes Horsley for his horror of nudity) of William Otter Gibbs, aged three, entitled *A Master of Hounds*. The precocious infant stands legs apart, Henry VIII-wise, like Reynolds' Master Crewe, holding a hunting-crop, whose long lash and thong curl round the step below him, while three shaggy dogs gaze up adoringly. The picture was appropriately chosen as a period piece (the 1880s) for the Treasure Houses of Britain Exhibition in Washington in 1985.

The lovely garden is almost entirely Major Gibbs's creation. Notable features are the circular Dutch cheese vats of copper which punctuate the ends of vistas, centres of lawns and lonely spaces, and are filled with flowering plants.

A Master of Hounds. William Otter Gibbs by John Horsley.

Snowshill Manor

Charles Paget Wade (1883-1956), who bought Snowshill Manor when it was semi-derelict in 1919, restored it, and gave it to the National Trust in 1951.

Opposite top: Snowshill Manor, William Sambach's Georgian front from the lower lawn. On the left is the Priest's House in which Charles Wade lived amongst a multitude of tools and gadgets.

Opposite left. Looking down on Armillary Court and late medieval dovecote, with 380 bird-boxes.

Opposite right. The front of the house from the entrance gates.

Snowshill is a small village about two miles to the south of Broadway. When I first knew the village the lane leading into it was a rutted and precipitous track with grass growing in the middle and three gates to open and shut. It was dreaded by motorists who in winter were often obliged to climb it in reverse. Indeed the village pronounced Snawesille, or Snozzle, lived, and still lives up to its name, for throughout the winter months, however green the grass in Broadway, Snawesille is invariably shouded by snow.

Until the Dissolution Snowshill Manor was the property of Winchcombe Abbey. Thereafter it never belonged to anyone of note, nor to anyone for long, until its last proprietor turned up. At the turn of the 18th century a William Sambach was lord of the manor and left his mark on the house. He tacked on a charming Queen Anne front to the earlier parts at the rear. In 1779 Rudder, county historian, wrote that, 'were the manor house in a better situation, it would be called handsome.' Instead it was practically inaccessible. It then belonged to an absentee gentleman, John Small of Clapham, Surrey, who let it as a farmhouse. In the 1820s the steward of Lord Wemyss' Stanway estate inhabited it. Again it became a farmhouse and in urgent need of repair. In 1919 a sapper in the Royal Engineers, stationed at Doullens in France saw an advertisement for Snowshill Manor in an old copy of *Country Life*. As soon as he got back to England he went to look at it one bleak day in February. He promptly bought it. Charles Paget Wade is surely the most remarkable person to have owned it; and it is his re-creation.

Wade was a scholar, architect (he designed several houses for the Hampstead Garden Suburb Trust), poet (indifferent), collector craftsman. He was a solitary and an eccentric. His appearance was extraordinary. Lutyens described him as 'a most remarkable creature, short with a face like a death mask of Henry Irving with a thick fuzz of grey hair, cut like a sponge.' I recall his hair as straight, parted in the middle and falling down to his shoulders, which was very unusual before the last War. He wore a stiff winged collar attached to a soft pleated shirt under a Norfolk jacket. He was always in breeches and stockings, and his shoes were adorned with large silver buckles. With his old wax complexion, angular features and sharp nose, his presence was daunting. But at heart he was a child. He admitted to Lutyens that he loved toys and had never grown up. He had a child's insatiable wonder and curiosity. He took nothing for granted. A tassel to him was an object deserving intense scrutiny and examination. How was it made, and of what, and by whom, and for what purpose? 'I am told his bravery in the [Great] War was phenomenal. He must be an "It"' Lutyens concluded, wrongly.

Because Wade was descended from a long line of sugar planters in St Kitts (his forebears had been engaged in litigation with William Beckford) he was rich enough to indulge his mania for collecting. He did not spend his money on works of art because they were rare or valuable but because their design, colour or workmanship pleased him. He began collecting at the age of 7, his first find being a little bone shrine of St. Michael (since stolen by a visitor) for 1/6d, the equivalent of 18 weeks pocket money.

Like the contents, the architecture of the house which enshrines them is an ambiguity of dates, very difficult to determine. Yet one may guess that from around 1400 additions had been made every hundred years until Sambach's extension in 1712 when the building of Snowshill Manor came to a full stop. Contrasting periods of architecture jostle together. Yet nothing conflicts. Of a uniform silvery grey stone the gables, chamfered mullion windows, chimney breasts and projecting porch room of the west front tone together in a traditional Cotswold whole. Detached from this front is a building called The Priest's House. The ground floor contains Wade's workshop, the floor covered and the ceiling suspended with the archaic tools of his trade. It is like an alchemist's cell. An enormous pair of blacksmith's bellows was operated by a cord attached to the porter's chair in which he habitually sat. Upstairs, approached by a winding stone staircase the magician slept in a cupboard-bed in the wall. To wash he was obliged to cross the open yard to a tap and basin in the main house.

Entrance to the manor is from the village through a pair of handsome stone piers between two little pavilions, or gazebos. They are intentionally overshadowed by trees so as to form a dense green vault in contrast to the open sunny forecourt beyond. A straight gravel path leads to Sambach's would-be classical front. Under an immensely high-pitched and stone-tiled roof the front door bears somewhat incongruously the Sambach arms within a primitive sort of pediment. The imperfect symmetry of the front, with four thick sash-barred windows to the left and five casement windows to the right, is engaging. The rooms behind the south front are, as one would expect, typical of the Queen Anne period with fielded panelling. All the rooms in the house have been given names by Charles Wade – Meridian, Admiral, Seraphim, Nadir, Dragon, and in the attics Top Gallant, Seventh Heaven and Hundred Wheels (filled with antique velocipedes).

Top. Snowshill Manor. Downstairs in the Priest's House. The hall porter's chair was Charles Wade's favourite seat.

Bottom. Dragon, derived from the fire nearly always kept burning. The room was the lower part of the medieval hall.

Every room is cluttered from floor to ceiling with furniture and curiosities, good and indifferent. All are rendered dark and mysterious by hung banners, tapestries and Turkish carpets. There are oak buffets, Spanish cabinets, chests, porters' chairs, Sedan chairs, Sicilian reliquaries, Chinese lacquer tables, clavicords and every species of musical instrument, navigational instruments and costumes (one of the finest costume collections in Great Britain). Yet, strange to relate, Wade wrote that 'a room with a multitude of objects can have a disquieting and restless atmosphere.' What he meant was that furniture should not be obtrusive, but should be subordinate to the room. Yet he loved high lights of gold, coloured marbles and polished metals on cabinets.

The Green Room is filled with models in Samurai armour, standing and seated before a sea of weapons. This macabre room was calculated to send children into fits of terror. Indeed Charles Wade's humour was, to put it mildly, sardonic. He richly enjoyed taking advantage of his visitors' distraction while he conducted them round the house. Unobserved he would disappear behind a tapestry into a secret passage to re-emerge beside them several minutes later in an upstairs room having changed into 18th century clothes, and resume his conversation as though no ghostly transmutation had happened. Or he might leap, with streaming hair, through the flames of a blazing fire to land at their feet.

Summer and winter the air inside the house was misty with pale blue smoke and redolent of wood log, mixed with the smell of joss-sticks, pomanders, medieval parchments, wormy book-bindings and decaying fabrics. Apart from the smouldering fires there was no form of heating whatever.

The pretty compartmented gardens were contrived by Wade from a plan drawn up by his friend, M. H. Baillie Scott, during the first three decades of the century. He defined them as 'an extension of the house, a series of outdoor rooms,' which afforded unbroken views of orchards and the sloping woods across the valley. He was more interested in layout than plantmanship; He detested cut flowers in the house. He preferred growing flowers, 'in which tones of blues, mauves and purples predominate; delphiniums, larkspur, lavender, with secondary use of salmons and creams, and sparing use of bright reds and yellows,' against a multiplicity of grey walls. He raised a series of terraces to mitigate a sense that the garden was sliding downhill into the valley. Consequently long flower borders intersect the terraces from the house to the dovecote at the bottom. The Armillary Court, with central column bears a gilded sundial; the lawned Well Court a Venetian well-head. Lavish use has been made of turquoise blue and gold on St George's bellcote, a figure of the Madonna, a zodiac clock and the garden gates and furniture.

My Garden sweet enclosed with walles strong
my arbours and alyes so pleasant and so dulce

Well Court has an ancient Venetian well-head.

Snowshill Manor, an aquatint by Charles Wade looking up at the west front of c. 1500. The gazebo room at the top of the steps added c. 1720.

is one of several slightly whimsy inscriptions painted by his own hand on gates and loggias to remind us that Charles Wade was a link with William Morris and the Pre-Raphaelites.

Late in life he married, to everyone's surprise, a lady many years younger than himself. In 1951 he presented Snowshill Manor to the National Trust, his earnest desire being that people should learn to appreciate and love good craftmanship from the curiosities he had assembled and the artefacts of his own skilled hands. He retired to the West Indies where he died in 1956. He is buried in Snowshill churchyard.

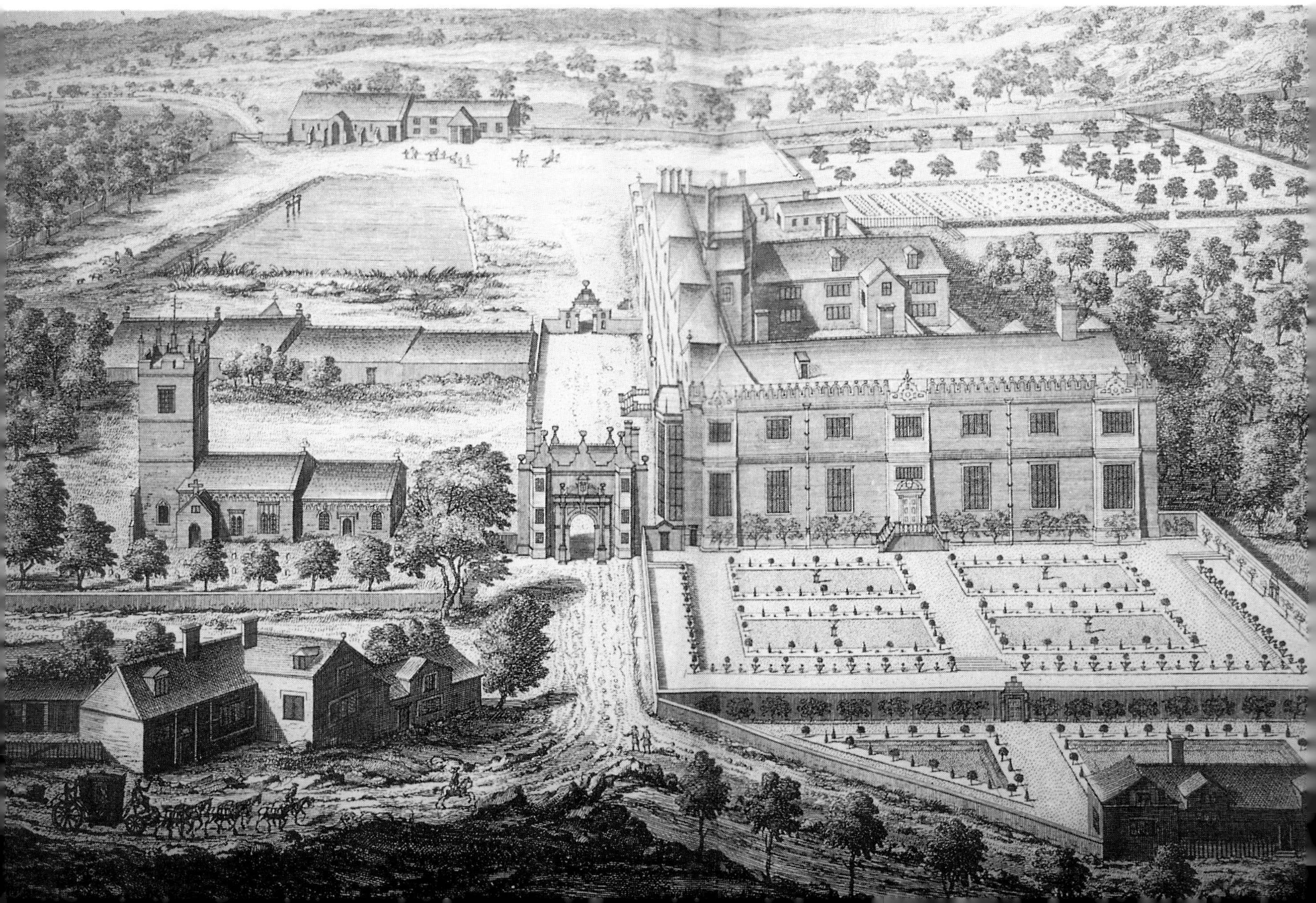

Stanway House

Stanway House. The Abbot of Tewkesbury's 14th century tithe barn and part of the west front of the house.

Top. Stanway House. The Elizabethan west front from the church tower and the Pyramid at the end of the vista.

Bottom. J. Kip's plate of Stanway in 1712, in which the surviving church, gatehouse, barn, north arch, west and south fronts are shown. Much of the north parts have been demolished.

Of how many country houses can it be said that they have changed hands once only since the 8th century, and that once from being monastic to domestic property? The record is made more marvellous when claimed by a country house incontestibly one of the most beautiful and romantic in the British Isles.

Stanway, meaning stony way, was a manor given to Tewkesbury Abbey on its foundation in 715 as sole endowment by a pair of Saxon brothers, of whom nothing is known beyond the absurdity of their names, Odo and Dodo. This was long before Gloucestershire was to contain more abbeys than any other county in England; hence the saying, 'As sure a God is in Gloucestershire.' Meanwhile four monks resided in what cannot have been more than a cell, praying for the souls of their benefactors, the egregious Odo and Dodo.

Today the motorist, leaving the main road from Broadway to Winchcombe and driving through a park of venerable trees will suddenly come upon a complex of buildings – medieval barn, Norman church, Jacobean gatehouse and Tudor manor-house – all of the same honey-coloured stone in an incomparable setting at the foot of a gentle escarpment. Nothing jars and everything delights. It is almost too good to be true, for there is not one unsightly thing to be seen.

Stanway was one of the first monastic establishments to be dissolved in Henry VIII's reign. The Tracy family of nearby Toddington kept a predatory eye on the monks' properties in the neighbourhood, including Winchcombe and Hailes abbeys. Sir William Tracy, puritanical by nature, anti-clerical in politics and a friend of William Tyndale, had a second son, Sir Richard to whom Stanway was granted in 1533. Richard was as radical as his father and played a sorry part in the dismantling of Hailes Abbey, actually seizing the greatly venerated vessel containing the Holy Blood of Christ and declaring it to be duck's blood tinted with saffron. The Tracys were a godless and ferocious breed, directly descended from William Tracy, one of the four knights who left Thomas à Becket hacked to pieces in Canterbury Cathedral. Legend maintains that his horse's hooves are heard clattering on the road on each anniversary of the knight's death in search of a priest to shrive his soul, though why Stanway, where he never lived, was chosen, has not been explained. No wonder the family were referred to by local people as 'The Tracys, the Tracys, the wind in their faces,' on whom and their successors a curse was laid by the dispossessed clerics of Stanway.

However reprehensible the part played by the Tracys in the destruction of two monasteries their replacements did not lack the aesthetic touch. The mansion they built at Hailes (long ago demolished) and that of Stanway bear witness to their architectural taste. Sir Richard Tracy however seems to have been too busy compiling anti-papistical tracts and combating superstitious abuses to engage in building. He was content to reside in the Abbot's 'fair stone house', or what remained of it at Stanway. In 1569 he was succeeded by his son Paul, who was created a baronet in 1611. Sir Paul was of less fanatical metal than his father and grandfather. He was the builder of the west front of the house facing the churchyard, from which it is best seen.

Stanway House, the Jacobean gatehouse, showing the north arch at the far end of the forecourt.

The long front under four well spaced and pointed gables with the immensely high oriel at the south end is of regular, if severe design. It ante-dates the gatehouse, by which one approaches it at a right-angle and which, with the north arch, forms a forecourt. The gatehouse, once rashly attributed to Inigo Jones, must date from James I's reign because Sir Paul died in 1625. This exquisite building is a curious mixture of late Gothic and renaissance motifs. The more one looks at its curvilinear gables, projecting bay windows, filigree balustrading and Mannerist centre-piece of fluted columns, broken pediment bearing a box-like panel with coat of arms, outsize scallop-shells (the Tracy crest) and pointed entrance, the more mongrel it appears. The north arch seen through the gatehouse is by comparison almost pure Baroque in its rustication, broken scrolled pediment and niches. The two are undoubtedly contemporary and were perhaps designed by Timothy Strong, owner of the famous quarries at Little Barrington and Taynton in Oxfordshire, and founder of a dynasty of master-masons. The ashlar stone of both gatehouse and north arch is slightly more orange than that of the west front, which is softened by centuries of silvery lichen, and according to Alec Clifton-Taylor came from Guiting over the hill.

If one passes across the forecourt and through the north arch one comes to the surprisingly pretty stable block built by that usually dreary Victorian architect, William Burn. These stables replaced those which had stood adjacent to the north wall of the churchyard; but the bad language of the strappers disconcerted the congregation during services, and they were pulled down. Set back to the left in the Abbot of Tewkesbury's 14th century tithe barn with a splendid stone roof supported by massive beams. The immensely wide entrance is from the north. The eccentric curved finials on the three gable ends are said to be cockscombs in reference to the dedication of Stanway church to St Peter and the thrice-crowing cock.

The stable block built by William Burn, 1859-1860.

The front door of the house leads straight into a screens passage with dining-room on the left, and great hall on the right. In the early 18th century a Doric colonnade was substituted for whatever Sir Paul had for a screen. The original hall ceiling pattern in compartments of beams laid alternately length- and width-wise was kept by Burn when renewing the woodwork. The flagged floor remains. The walls are hung with hatchments in place of 'all the signs of antiquity, of muskets and swords,' observed by Anne Rushout in 1809. Against the west wall is an oak shuffle-board table, the top all of one piece, over 22 ft long and nearly 3ft wide with original brass counters and end tray. It is mentioned in an inventory of 1735 as being in the hall – indeed it could not possibly be got out whole – and dates from about 1620 having been cut from a tree planted about 1350. From the dais end rises the astonishing oriel, the height of the room. Lady Cynthia Asquith referred in her diaries to the evening light filtering through the oriel, 'with hundreds [actually there are 1,036] latticed panes, so mellowed by time that whenever the sun shines through their amber and green glass, the effect is of a vast honeycombe and indeed at all times and in all weathers of stored sunshine.'

The late-Stuart south front built for Sir Humphrey Tracy.

Sir Paul Tracy's grandson, Sir Humphrey who succeeded as 3rd baronet in 1657, probably built the long south wing at right angles to the hall, thus turning the house into an L. I say *probably* because there is no documentary proof beyond stylistic evidence. The south front is more ingenious than might at first sight be supposed. Viewed from outside it is of two storeys in height, perfectly symmetrical and level, whereas on looking through an arch from the hall one sees the enfilade of rooms rising in a series of steps. In other words the levels of the rooms behind the widely spaced windows are unequal. Although so different from Sir Paul's west front, which is vertical, the horizontal south front is distinguished by similar mullion windows, by strapwork crestings and a minutely arcaded parapet, all of which proclaim late Jacobean or early Caroline provenance. The lead downpipes, like those on the west front, were put up by Sir Humphrey's son and heir, Sir Richard, 4th baronet, in 1670. The beautiful south doorway is an afterthought of 1724.

The drawing-room, which can be approached up seven steps from the dais end of the hall, likewise took its present form in 1724. It has early Georgian panelling and doorheads and a rather simple fireplace flanked by grand fluted pilasters. The Jacobean-style plaster ceiling is clearly a Victorian addition. In this room are the most notable pieces of furniture in the house, namely an unusual, if not unique pair of Chinosierie sofas with pagoda testers and bells, made about 1760 for Amisfield House, East Lothian, the seat of the 7th Earl of Wemyss.

Sir John Tracy (who had inherited from his nephew) dying in 1678 without children was the last baronet. He left Stanway to his cousin Ferdinando, the younger son of the 3rd Viscount Tracy of Toddington. So Stanway continued in Tracy descent from Sir Richard, Henry VIII's grantee of the estate, until the death of Ferdinando's grandson Anthony, who had assumed the surname of Keck, through Ferdinando's heiress wife. In 1769 Anthony left two daughters of whom the elder Henrietta-Charlotte, Viscountess Hereford, lived out her long widowhood at Stanway, and the younger Susan was married to Lord Elcho, son of the 7th Earl of Wemyss.

Life at Stanway in Lady Hereford's day must have been rather melancholy. She had no children and although she was a Maid of Honour to Queen Charlotte, seems seldom to have left home. Anne Rushout wrote that she lived in one fairly comfortable room hung with old family portraits in a house that was 'dismally placed'. Lady Hereford adored her dogs and lamented their deaths. When her favourite Mignon, of whom she had a portrait taken, died she ordered him to be buried in a place unknown to her so that she should could not mourn over the grave, and wrote a poignant little eulogy to be enclosed in the coffin: 'He died the 27 September 1807 to her extream Agony. He was of exquisite and most uncommon beauty, with a peculiar elegance of motion, very small. I have suffered much in writing this paper.' She beseeched whosoever might come upon the coffin, or box, to replace her eulogy. This cannot have been done since the paper is now kept in the house.

On Lady Hereford's death in 1817 Susan Lady Elcho came into possession and Stanway passed to her descendants. Susan and Henrietta-Charlotte's other claim to fame is to have had a great-great-grandmother painted with a bluebottle on her left breast. The portrait is in the house. In 1883 the 10th Earl of Wemyss made Stanway over to his son Hugo Lord Elcho on his marriage to Mary Wyndham, the Earl retaining his Scottish seat, Gosford in East Lothian. During their married life (both died in 1937) the Elchos made Stanway a centre of that intellectual and artistic coterie known as The Souls, of which Mary Elcho (she became Lady Wemyss) was the beloved cynosure. The Souls, of whom her brother George Wyndham, Lord Curzon, Violet Duchess of Rutland, Harry Cust, Lady Desborough (mother of the Grenfell brothers), Maurice Baring and Arthur Balfour were members, constantly visited Stanway. Surrounded by her adorers and children as bright and intellectual as herself, the absent-minded Lady Weymss reigned supreme, attended by the Rev. H. B. Allen, a sort of Hogarthian chaplain, but in fact Vicar of Stanway and Didbrook, dottily eccentric, a believer in free love and devotee of whisky, always insolvent in spite of cramming the *jeunesse dorée*, and perhaps because of making his vicarage a home for sick donkeys and horses. Yet because her husband, ultimately the 11th Earl, was an incorrigible spendthrift, Stanway during these 55 years was always a little down at heel. Lady Cynthia Asquith recalled

Above. Double portrait (? by Daniel de Koninck) of Robert Tracy (1706-1767) M.P., who inherited Stanway, and John Tracy (later Atkyns, later Keck, 1706-1773). The elder of these identical twins had a red ribbon tied round his wrist to distinguish his identity.

Opposite top. Stanway House, the east front.

Opposite below. Panoramic view by William Taylor of Worcester of the east front, showing the Canal curiously distorted.

that the memories of her childhood home were permanently overcast by financial worries, and that she and her brothers and sisters were brought up in a state of 'spartan luxury'.

Mary Wemyss' sitting-room in the east corner of the west wing, with her portrait by Poynter, her father Percy Wyndham's by Lord Leighton, her son Elcho's (he was killed in the Great War) and his wife Lady Violet Manners' by Sargent, with other relics and treasures makes a nostalgic little museum of a recent but totally vanished phase of British civilization.

Soon after the 11th Earl's death came the Second World War, to be followed by post-war austerity and all the accompanying menaces to a large estate it implied. But during the past 8 years Stanway has been lived in by James Charteris, Lord Neidpath, to whom his father the present Earl of Wemyss made it over. By sheer good husbandry and tactful demolition of unneeded back premises he has made the estate and house what is called a 'viable proposition.' Moreover he has in mind plans for further improvements. His wife Catherine Guinness shares his intellectual interests, and once again Stanway has become the nucleus of a new coterie of intellect and art.

Mary Wyndham, Lady Elcho (later Lady Wemyss), 1862-1937, by Sir E. J. Poynter.

One of Lord Neidpath's schemes is to restore the great canal which, until it was drained and filled in, stretched along the hillside between the house and a belvedere, called the Pyramid. This object still dominates the landscape from the hill's summit, and is reached from the south lawn by a clearing between two belts of trees. Amongst the trees is a tiny circular dog cemetary, enclosed by a hedge, where Lord Neidpath has raised a gravestone whose epitaph, beneath a tin of dog food and crossed bones, begins: 'Memoriae fragranti OLD SMELLY.'

The belvedere's architect is unknown, but a plaque records that it was built in 1750 by Robert Tracy, gentleman, in memory of his father. From it, a cascade once gushed downhill over ramps into the canal. The canal is not shown in Kip's engraving of 1712 but appears in a primitive painting of 1748 by William Taylor, a Worcester brass founder. From the Pyramid lovely views are had of Oxenton, Alderton, Dumbleton and Bredon hills, the further Malverns and the distant Black Mountains of Wales.

The Pyramid, built by Robert Tracy (elder of the twins) in memory of his father, John Tracy, in 1750.

Memorial to Old Smelly.

Sudeley Castle

Ideally Sudeley Castle should first be seen from above. This need not cause difficulty because it lies, like so many of the best old Cotswold houses in a coombe of the long escarpment which stretches from Lansdown, near Bath, to Meon Hill. From a disstance it appears a turreted, embattled mass of butter-coloured stone, all of a piece and seemingly all of a period, which of course is not the case.

For nearly two centuries the Castle stood a ghostly ruin after it was dismantled by Oliver Cromwell. The prosperous citizens of Winchcombe town, one short mile away, systematically treated it as a quarry from which to build houses for themselves. The deserted and despoiled castle was a favourite haunt of artists, antiquarians and just the idly curious. John Byng, the diarist, had as usual much to complain of – the badness of the road from Winchcombe, 'a mean, dirty, market-town' – and something to praise, surprisingly, in the magnificence of the ruins.

Sudeley Castle. The Inner Courtyard with ruins of the Banquetting Hall and the Outer Courtyard beyond.

Sudeley's history has been long and much associated with kings and queens. Its first owner was Ethelred the Unready who gave it to his daughter Goda, the sister of Edward the Confessor. Her descendants held it until the time of Sir Thomas Boteler, an illustrious admiral in the wars against the French. In 1441 he began to build the present fabric. On the death however of his master Henry VI he fell foul of that monarch's successor and was obliged to forfeit the castle to Edward IV. Again Sudeley became royal property until the young King Edward VI granted it to his rapacious uncle, Sir Thomas Seymour, Lord High Admiral of England and younger brother of the Protector Duke of Somerset.

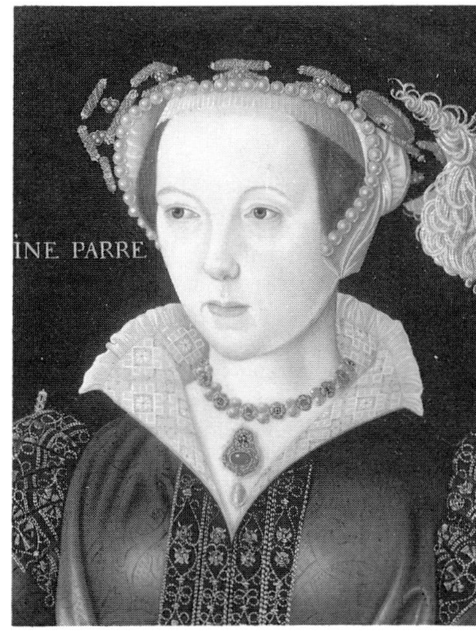

Queen Katherine Parr who married Sir Thomas Seymour of Sudeley in 1547 and died in 1548. Attrib. to W. Scrots c. 1545.

Thomas Seymour was a seductive rotter. He secretly married Queen Katherine Parr only three months after the death of her husband Henry VIII in 1547. She was a kind and gentle soul. She not only protected her step-daughters, the future Queens Mary and Elizabeth, from their father's terrifying tantrums, but likewise the ill-fated Lady Jane Grey whom she took to live with her at Sudeley. Katherine's residence at Sudeley was brief and unhappy. While Thomas was absent philandering with other ladies, including Princess Elizabeth, she gave birth to a daughter in September 1548. A few days later she died of puerperal fever, protesting to the end against her husband's harsh treatment. She was buried in the lovely little chapel built by Boteler a few yards north of the castle. Even so she was not allowed to rest undistrubed. In 1782 her grave was dug up and her corpse, wrapped in seven layers of cerecloth, examined and dissected by busybodies. It is gratifying to learn that one of them was made physically sick by the stench of the foetid remains.

Queen Katherine Parr's Room.

A year only after Katherine's death her ambitious husband, having attempted to turn Edward VI against the Protector and marry the young king to Jane Grey, was charged with high treason and very properly executed. So too was poor innocent Lady Jane five years later.

In 1554 the castle was granted by the Crown to the Brydges family, who became Viscounts Chandos of Sudeley. The 6th Viscount fought for Charles I who stayed at the castle during the Civil War. In 1644 it was besieged and surrendered to the Parliamentarians. Four years later it was 'slighted'.

In 1830 two brothers, John and William Dent, glove-makers from Worcester, fell in love with the castle and its history. Having bought it they devoted the remainder of their lives to restoring, decorating and filling it with what they considered appropriate furniture and relics. They used the local stone to match that of the old existing walls. The restoration and additions were carried out with remarkable tact by the eminent Gothic architect, Sir George Gilbert Scott. Work went on until 1854 when the younger brother William Dent died. The elder, John, was broken-hearted. A local newspaper recorded the harrowing death scene. 'Their mutual love and esteem were as warm and true as in the days of their boyhood and youth, so now their separation by death was all the more painful. The one word uttered by each was "Brother!" Then, locked in each other's arms, there was something in the parting of these two dear old men too sacred and too touching to be witnessed by others, and all silently withdrew.' The author claimed that Dickens to a large extent drew the brothers Dent in the Cheeryble brothers of *Nicholas Nickleby*.

Still the restoration of Sudeley went on. The brothers' nephew and his wife, born Emma Brocklehurst, worked like Trojans to make the greater part of the castle habitable. Emma was a grand and splendid lady who, when widowed, continued to dedicate her life to Sudeley, buying and collecting paintings, manuscripts and anything relating to its past history that she could lay her hands on. When she died childless in 1900 she left the property to a nephew of her own, Henry, who prefixed the name of Dent to Brocklehurst. His great-grandson is the present representative of the Dent-Brocklehurst family. Mr. Dent-Broklehurst's mother Elizabeth and her second husband Lord Ashcombe live in the castle which is regularly open to the public.

Roughly speaking Sudeley Castle consists of narrow ranges of buildings round two large adjacent courtyards, of which the south is open to the garden. The walls of the so-called Outer (north) Courtyard, except for Boteler's gatehouse, date from the mid-and late-1500s; those of the Inner Courtyard from the 1400s. In the latter the High Presence Chamber remains roofless and floorless, its great, gaunt windows facing a Tudor herb garden with fountain.

The Tudor Succession by Hans Eworth. Composite portraits of Henry VIII, Queen Mary and Philip II of Spain and Queen Elizabeth.

The castle from the north-west.

The long eastern ranges of both courtyards are open to the public, the rooms filled mostly with the Dent brothers' and Emma Dent's collections. The family's separate apartments occupy the western and the north ranges of the Outer Courtyard as far as the Gatehouse. Within the last few years they have been skilfully refurbished by Lady Ashcombe. Of the Dents' 19th-century decoration precious little survives, including the roofs. The new rooms are extremely elegant, filled with important paintings from Lady Ashcombe's mother-in-law's family, the Morrisons, and treasures inherited by Lord Ashcombe from his grandmother, Mrs George Keppel.

The castle is very much a living and even thriving concern. Over and above the wing occupied by the family, and the apartments regularly open to visitors, the 15th century block at the south-west end of the Inner Courtyard down to the Dungeon Tower, is now given over to craft workshops whose occupants all come from Winchcombe and the immediate neighbourhood. The shops produce stained glass, marbled paper, leather goods, turnery ware, joinery and furniture painting. Thus Lady Ashcombe has revived some of the traditional Cotswold skills which were only waiting to be revived by someone with initiative and enthusiasm.

The lovely garden, of which the raised and balustraded terrace was made by the Dents, overlooks fields of pasture and the Winchcombe hills beyond. Hedges of yew, shaped like bastioned walls, and isolated yew trees like bee-hives are reminiscent of Gertrude Jekyll's style of topiary. Boteler's Chapel, a fine specimen of Perpendicular architecture was roofed, paved and pewed by Scott between 1859 and 1863. In the chancel a tomb with effigy, exquisitely carved by J. B. Philip, were provided for the desecrated remains of Henry VIII's last Queen Consort, who although fortunate to survive her first marriage, had little more than a year and a half to regret her second. Boteler's Great Barn, buttressed but still roofless, is a noble old relic in the east quarter of the garden.

St. Mary's Chapel, built c. 1460 and restored by Sir George Gilbert Scott, 1859-63. Queen Katherine Parr is buried in the chapel.

Acknowledgements

The Dovecote Press is grateful to the following for allowing the use of illustrations in their possession: Guy Acloque Esq, 19. Mrs. Jonathan Blow, 97, 101 (bottom). Mrs. Alan Clutton-Brook, 48 (top), 51, 52, 53 (top), 53 (bottom). Robert Cooper Esq, 14. Major Martin Gibbs, 137, 139 (bottom), 141. The Hon. Mrs. Derek Jackson, 36 (top), 38. Nicholas Mander Esq, 120, 121 (top). Mrs. Laurence Rook, 43. By permission of the Earl Bathurst, photographs Cortauld Institute of Art, 59, 60. By permission of the Duke of Beaufort, photographs Cortauld Institute of Art, 20 (top), 20 (centre). By permission of Lord Neidpath, photographs Cortauld Institute of Art, 152, 153 (bottom), 154 (top). *Country Life*, 23, 26, 28 (top), 28 (bottom left), 28 (bottom right), 31, 32, 33, 77, 79, 98 (bottom), 99 (top), 100, 121 (centre), 126 (top), 126 (bottom), 127, 128 (top), 128 (top right), 128 (bottom), 133 (centre), 134, 135. *The Daily Telegraph*, 139 (bottom). The National Portrait Gallery, 15, 156 (top). The National Trust, 111, 143, 145 (top), 145 (bottom), 147.

A special debt is owing to Anthony Kersting Esq for his skill and patience in providing the following photographs: Frontispiece, 10, 13 (top), 17 (top), 25 (top), 27, 34 (top), 34 (bottom), 37 (top), 37 (bottom), 49, 54 (top), 56 (top), 56 (bottom), 57 (top), 57 (bottom), 58, 61 (top), 74, (top), 74 (bottom), 80, 81, 82, 83, 84 (top), 84 (bottom), 86, 87, 101 (top), 102, 104, 105, 106 (top), 106 (bottom), 107, 113, 114, 115, 116, 117, 118 (top), 118 (bottom), 121 (bottom), 122 (top), 122 (bottom), 130 (top), 130 (bottom), 136, 155, 156 (bottom), 157, 158 (top), 158 (bottom).

The remaining photographs were taken by David Burnett, who would like to thank the owners of the houses for their considerable support and cooperation.